Surviving and Thriving on the Single-Parent Journey

A Step-by-Step Approach

D1068550

Surviving and Thriving on the Single-Parent Journey

A Step-by-Step Approach

Kat Seney-Williams

LION

Published by
Lion Hudson Limited
Wilkinson House, Jordan Hill Business Park
Banbury Road, Oxford OX2 8DR, England
www.lionhudson.com

ISBN 978 0 7459 8058 4
e-ISBN 978 0 7459 8059 1

First edition 2019

Acknowledgments
The quotation on page 108 is reproduced by kind permission of Sue Carpenter, writer and documentary maker www.suecarpenter.co.uk.

A catalogue record for this book is available from the British Library

Printed and bound in the UK, July 2019, LH26

CONTENTS

PART 4 The climb uphill: getting equipped for the journey

To all the single parents out there of all shapes, sizes and backgrounds – you are not alone!

ACKNOWLEDGMENTS

I would like to thank the many single parents who shared their stories with me – for some of you I know this wasn't easy.

Thank you to my family, whom I love so much. My children, Cheyenne and Steven, who walked with me on the journey – we made it to the end and I am so proud of you both. My husband Jordan, the man who waited for me patiently, loving me unconditionally until I was ready to give love a second chance – you have won my heart. My grandson Cobi – you have brought so much joy into our lives. My parents, Shirley and Clifford: Dad, you have always been there for me and taught me by your example to work hard and persevere; Mom, you are no longer with us, but your influence still impacts my life to this day. My brother Rick and sister-in-law Sherry, who flew across an ocean to be there for me when my life was in turmoil – you offered me hope. And to the rest of my family – our trips to see you after I became a single parent were a healing balm poured out over our hearts.

Thank you to my friends, especially Gillian, Rachel, Cher, Rosie, Jill, James and Phil who were there for me through all the ups and downs, and to Mary, a fellow author and friend.

To Alison Hull, who saw a story and a passion within me and was the first to encourage me to write this book – I am grateful to you. To the team at Lion Hudson – thank you for your hard work in bringing this book to publication. And thank you to my wonderful colleagues at Care for the Family for your encouragement and support, especially Sheron Rice, who edited this book – you are amazing at what you do, made sense of my waffling, and brought it together so beautifully.

And last but not least, thank you to God my Father, who walked with me, sometimes carrying me, every step of the way.

FOREWORD

"Single parenting is parenting for marines!" I first heard that phrase a couple of years ago and it's a brilliant metaphor. I honestly believe that single parents have one of the hardest jobs on the face of the earth.

Over the years I've had many memorable conversations with parents, but some of the ones that have stayed with me longest are those I've had with single parents. I remember the mum who cried as she told me about the terrible pain she felt after her partner left and how she was struggling to cope with her feelings of anger, grief, rejection, and, sometimes, sheer bewilderment. There was the mum who lived in fear of getting the flu or having to go into hospital, because she didn't know who would care for her children. And there was the dad who told me that even doing ordinary things seemed like climbing a mountain. I heard about families living hand-to-mouth and parents worrying that they weren't able to give their children things that other kids had. One mum seemed to encapsulate so much of the isolation single parents can feel when she told me: "There's nobody at home to say, 'Don't be daft' or 'Let the baby cry for a while' or 'You're doing a great job'. I so often have the sense that I really am on my own."

That's why in our work at Care for the Family we make it one of our priorities to support single parents. One of the things I am most proud of is the Take a Break holidays for single-parent families that we've run for over twenty-five years. These subsidised activity breaks offer single parents the opportunity to have lots of fun with their children, try exciting new activities, create lasting memories, and make new friends. Mums and dads who have been on one of these holidays tell us that it's a time when they can relax in the knowledge that they are among people who understand what it's like to be parenting on your own.

We were delighted when Kat Seney-Williams, the author of this book, joined us a few years ago to be our Single Parent Support Coordinator. A lone parent herself for many years, Kat is passionate about supporting other single parents, and I am thrilled that she has written this book. She shares a wealth of advice about raising children and navigating the realities of parenting alone, co-parenting and non-resident parenting.

As Kat travels your single-parent journey with you, her hope and mine is that you will find this book not only full of practical help and encouragement, but most of all that it will lead you to a future filled with hope.

ROB PARSONS, OBE
CHAIRMAN AND FOUNDER OF CARE FOR THE FAMILY

Part 1

The beginning of the journey

Chapter 1

ENTRY POINTS

....

I never thought it would happen to me.

KAT

On a cold winter's night in the heart of the Adirondack Mountains, the man of my dreams asked me to go for a walk with him. We made our way up the road hand in hand, and as we reached the top, he brought us to a stop. We gazed into each other's eyes while the snow fell peacefully around us, glistening in the moonlight. All we could hear was the whistling of the wind blowing through the tall pine trees. It was in this beautiful setting that I was asked for my hand in marriage. The atmosphere was electric, and my heart and mind were full of hope for the future. It was all so perfect – a fairy tale.

Fifteen years later, I stood in the hallway of our house watching my husband as he picked up his bags and walked out the door. He never came back.

To this day, I can remember how I felt as I watched him leave. My emotions were some of the most painful I have ever experienced. All that I had invested in over the past fifteen years came crashing down around me. I'd left everything I knew – my family, my studies at university, and my country (I moved from the States to the UK) – to be with the man who had promised to love and be with me until death parted us. I felt completely abandoned.

Every single parent has a unique story, so yours will be different from mine. Some of us planned to be single parents, but for most of us, it's not something we intended to happen and it may even have come about because of a crisis: we may have been bereaved, left an abusive relationship or had a one-night stand; our partner may have left us, we may have been cheated on, or we may even have been raped. I have never come across a single parent who said that when they were young they daydreamed about how great it would be to raise their children on their own one day. Most of our dreams were only ever about the "happily ever after". We have different entry points, but for most of us, single parenthood is an unexpected journey.

I thought that my marriage was fine. I mean, yes, we had our ups and downs, but what marriage doesn't, right? One day, out of the blue, my wife pulled me aside and told me that she didn't love me any more and that she was leaving me. I was in total shock. She left me to look after our three children alone.

JOHN

The day started like any other day. I was happily married with four beautiful children aged three, five, seven, and eight. My husband had gone off to the gym like he normally did, but this time he was away longer than usual. The phone rang, and my heart sank as I was given the news that my husband had collapsed and been taken to hospital by ambulance. I was told that he had a bleed on his brain and needed surgery. The doctor said his chances of survival were very slim and that if he got through the operation, he'd be in hospital for years and may not be the same person. John did make it through the operation but was then in a coma for a week before he passed away aged thirty-three.

REBECCA

On Monday morning I woke up, got the children ready for school, and headed off to work as normal. My husband stayed at home to get some odd jobs done around the house. At 3.45 p.m. I received a phone call. It was the start of my worst nightmare. I was told there was a problem concerning the family and that I needed to leave work immediately. I was taken to social services and told that my daughter had made allegations that she'd been molested by her father. I was in total shock! My husband had been arrested earlier that day and was subsequently put on trial, convicted, and sent to prison. There was never any doubt in my mind about divorcing my husband as I could never be with someone who would abuse their own daughter in such a way.

KELLY

I grew up believing that children should come after marriage and wanted this to be the case in my own life. After going out with a guy for a few months, I discovered I was pregnant at twenty. I was devastated, to say the least! What made it worse was knowing that I didn't want to marry him, even though he wanted to do the right thing by me. I contemplated running away, and all sorts of other things, rather than face up to the consequences. After a huge internal struggle, I decided I had to take responsibility for my actions. I gave birth to my beautiful daughter at the age of twenty-one. She has been a gift to me, and I'm so thankful I've got her.

JESS

Looking back, things were never really right between us. The emotional abuse started straight away, but I didn't recognize it at the time. When my ex-husband proposed to me, he insisted we went out late to celebrate, even though I wasn't feeling well and was jet-lagged. Things got steadily worse over the years, with physical abuse coming alongside the emotional abuse. Starting a family made him even worse. It was only when I discovered the Freedom programme through Children's Services that a chink of light got in and slowly began to reveal the truth about the man I had married and how abusive he was. I thank God I had the help of different organizations, family, and friends to help me leave him in as safe a way as I could. Life is easier now. I am not living with the daily erosion of my self-esteem any more, but we are still living in the aftermath of a very difficult period.

CARRIE

Our society has been guilty of creating a single-parent stereotype – a very young adult who does not want to work and has children in order to stay on benefits – but it is completely inaccurate. Single parents come from an array of backgrounds, ages, educational and earning levels, jobs and professions. Statistics show that 68 per cent of single parents work, their average age is thirty-nine, and less than 1 per cent are teenagers.[1] The reality is that single parents include people who are in education to gain better qualifications and enhance their prospects, people with demanding jobs, people looking after children at home, often because they cannot afford the costs of childcare, and people caring for their disabled children.

---

1   Rabindrakumar, S., "One in Four: A Profile of Single Parents in the UK", Gingerbread, February 2018. www.gingerbread.org.uk/wp-content/uploads/2018/02/One-in-four-a-profile-of-single-parents-in-the-UK.compressed.pdf

Many single parents feel isolated and different from other families, but in the UK alone there are 1.7 million single parents who are their children's primary caregivers.[2] Many others parent from a distance or co-parent. So, although our circumstances may be very different, as single parents we are certainly not alone on the journey.

It's a journey that has many ups and downs, and we'll be at different stages on it. Some parts are harder than others, and one of the things I most want to emphasize in this book is that we need to be gentle with ourselves – mentally, emotionally and physically. Single parenting is often said to be one of the hardest tasks a person can do in life, and we need to take things one step at a time.

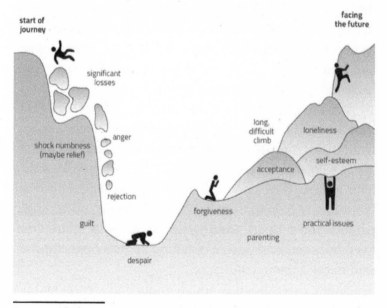

start of journey

facing the future

significant losses

long, difficult climb

loneliness

shock numbness (maybe relief)

anger

acceptance

self-esteem

rejection

forgiveness

practical issues

guilt

parenting

despair

---

2   Ibid.

I hope you'll allow me to travel with you on your single-parent journey. I want to help you come to terms with the past and give you hope and encouragement to face the challenges ahead. I have found the illustration shown on the previous page helpful in depicting the experiences you are likely to face. As you'll see, there may be steep climbs to negotiate, and at times you may feel like the despairing person at the very bottom of the valley. But be prepared to find yourself re-visiting certain stages and parenting issues, as the journey may not be as linear as the illustration suggests. At these times it may feel as though you're taking two steps forward and one back.

When starting any journey, it's essential to equip yourself for it – proper clothing and footwear, food and drink, a compass and a map – and the aim of this book is to help you be fully equipped for the single-parent journey. At first these will be baby steps, but then you'll take longer and longer strides until the day comes when you'll look back and not believe how far you have come.

I made plenty of mistakes on my own journey (and learned from them), but I also experienced successes and triumphs – it really is a rollercoaster ride. And no matter how much some of us may wish it was a journey we didn't have to take, if we choose to meet the challenges head on (with plenty of help from our friends, family, other single parents, and support groups), we can not only rebuild our lives, but even find ourselves taking up new opportunities we'd never dreamed of before.

Single parenthood is not all doom and gloom, and it's not just about *surviving*; it's about *thriving*. Yes, you heard me right: *thriving*. I'm not going to lie. For many of us, the fall at the start of the journey is hard and painful. But sooner or later, we'll begin the climb uphill – the climb to the top.

Chapter 2

OVERWHELMING EMOTIONS

The day my ex-husband left our marriage is permanently etched on my memory. For most people, it simply came and went, but for me it was the day my life changed for ever. I'll never forget standing in the kitchen doorway looking down the hall as he picked up his belongings and walked out the door. I was broken-hearted.

If we've become single parents because of a crisis, we'll be hit by an onslaught of emotions. This is perfectly normal, of course, but nonetheless these feelings can be overwhelming and scary. I remember feeling like a rabbit caught in headlights – stunned. It was as if I was watching a movie about my life; I just couldn't get my head around the fact that what was happening was for real.

....

I felt so shocked and very much wanted to have him
back with me and the children.

ANNA

I felt like it wasn't really happening to me, that it was surreal.

LUKE

When we have an emotional crisis or trauma our bodies respond by going into psychological shock. Physical symptoms may include insomnia or nightmares, fatigue, being easily startled, having difficulty concentrating, a racing heartbeat, edginess and agitation, muscle tension, an upset stomach, sweating, and aches and pains. Emotional symptoms may include denial or disbelief, confusion, anger, irritability, mood swings, anxiety, fear, guilt, shame, self-blame, withdrawal from others, feeling sad or hopeless, and feeling disconnected or numb.

It's common to want to keep talking over and over again about what has happened, so do speak to family and trusted friends. And if you don't have anyone you feel you can talk to, please don't bear things in silence. See the appendix for details of organizations that will offer a listening ear.

Numbness and denial

One of the main feelings of emotional shock can be a sense of numbness or even indifference. It's also not unusual for people to operate on autopilot – automatically doing routine things such as taking the children to school, feeding them, washing their clothes, and going to work. People around us may think we are "taking it well" or "being so brave" and have little or no idea what is really happening with us on an emotional level – there are feelings below the surface that are waiting to erupt.

I was in a state of shock for several weeks. It felt like it was happening to someone else. I was just watching everything unravel as if it was on a TV show.

JENNA

In the early days, all I remember doing was crying an awful lot.

PAM

The children and I just cried ourselves to sleep for several nights after my ex walked out.

JANET

This was something that happened to other people, not me. I was very hurt that someone so close could betray me and move on as though the sixteen years we'd shared (including having two boys) was so easily replaceable!

PAUL

When my marriage ended, I initially felt numb about everything and then I became very emotional. I would cry myself to sleep and wake up crying (I hadn't known that was humanly possible!) I couldn't talk about it to anyone without being tearful and used to feel so embarrassed, apologizing to my friends. However, for me, crying was the best medicine and my friends understood that; it was a way of coping and releasing all the hurt I was experiencing.

Disbelief soon followed shock. I wanted my family to stay together and believed with all my heart that something would change things around again. It took me so long to accept reality – the alternative was too painful. I was a fighter, and I didn't want to give in to the idea of there being no hope of keeping our family together.

Happiness and relief

For some of us, single parenthood is something we deliberately planned for. We may have longed for a child for many months or years and now, perhaps through adoption or artificial insemination, we have a precious son or daughter, and it is a time of celebration.

I chose to be a single parent and since finally having a child, I've just felt joy.

HAYLEY

Others of us are relieved and happy for a very different reason: we've come out of an abusive or unhappy relationship and now realize that we and our children are safe. We can start to live our lives again with hope.

Suddenly I felt I could breathe. I realized I'd been holding my breath for years.

DONNA

I felt a weight lifting from my shoulders. Same for the children. People commented that they appeared happy rather than looking haunted.

JASON

The abuse was so bad, but it took me years to plan my escape. I was so relieved when I got away.

DENISE

The immediate feeling was relief – relief that we weren't lying to each other any more and pretending to be happy.

PAUL

But even those of us who are relieved after leaving an abusive or unhappy relationship can be in a state of shock. We may start questioning ourselves about what we could have done differently or why we didn't leave earlier than we did. Those who have lived with domestic abuse often have very distressing emotions, and if this is your experience I would urge you to seek the help of a professional, such as a doctor or counsellor, to get you through this. Please don't suffer in silence.

Helplessness and hopelessness

One of the hardest and most painful things for me following the break-up of my marriage was seeing the pain it caused my children and not being able to take that away. Like all parents, I was used to being my children's "fixer", but now my hands were completely tied as I watched them grieve. The night after my ex-husband left, I remember sitting at the end of my son's bed, trying to comfort him until he fell asleep. The image of the hurt in his eyes will stay with me for ever. The world my children and I had known was crashing down around us and I felt helpless; there was nothing I could do to take the pain away.

Not only did I feel helpless, but I had an overwhelming feeling of hopelessness. The future seemed so bleak – I couldn't bear to even think about it. I know now that those kinds of thoughts are normal, but the truth is that the future we envisage is a distortion of the reality. In time, we will move on and be able to build a new life for our children and ourselves.

Whenever I meet single parents who are at this stage of their journey, I urge them to take every opportunity they can to talk to people who offer a listening ear. Talking things over with others not only helps us get all sorts of thoughts and feelings off our chest, but it can bring objectivity and a different perspective of the future. A conversation I had with my brother Rick had a lasting impact on my life when he came over from America to visit me. He could see how hurt, upset, and hopeless I was, and he told me that my life *wasn't* at an end – things would not always feel so bad. He planted the thought that I could embark on a new beginning. At the time, it didn't really sink in, but over the following days and weeks, as I slowly started to rebuild my life, I realized he was right. To this day, I am so grateful that he and my sister-in-law loved me enough to fly over 3,500 miles to spend that week with me after my ex-husband left. My brother's words sowed a little seed of hope in me that grew over time into a huge oak tree.

Accepting reality, one step at a time

Our minds and bodies can take around four weeks to work through the effects of shock if we have gone through a traumatic incident. Emotionally we are vulnerable, and we should not be afraid to turn to family or friends who are able to give us support. I learned from experience that I needed to take one day at a time, try not to run before I could walk, and not expect too much of myself.

Even when the denial stage has passed, it's easy for single parents to remain in a kind of limbo, not fully accepting reality. Perhaps we hang on to past relationships with the hope that things will change. I found it incredibly difficult to accept that my marriage was really over, because nothing happened for such a long time after my ex-husband left the family home. We weren't making any concrete decisions about our relationship, and certainly for my ex-husband it seemed easier just to let things drift – neither trying to reconcile nor seeking a divorce. Eventually, I knew that for the sake of my own sanity I had to put the wheels in motion to enable those important decisions to be made. Once I did that, I felt empowered to move forward with my life.

My family and friends were gentle with me and allowed me to walk at my own pace, but others can have a different experience. Sometimes well-meaning family or friends can push us to fly before we can even walk. If that is happening, it's important to be honest and tell those concerned that we're not yet ready to make that step. We need to move at a pace that is comfortable for *us*.

Perhaps you have been living in denial for some time now, just as I was, and maybe it's time to take that first step towards coming to terms with reality. It is a big step, and it can be scary, but remember that you won't be alone as you do this; you'll be joining the millions of other single parents who are on the journey already.

One of the aims of our Single Parent Support initiative at Care for the Family is to support each other so that we travel the journey together, so please do look us up on our website, and there are other organizations that specifically work to help single-parent families (see appendix for further details).

Chapter 3

LOSS

After an earthquake is over, victims will slowly gather their senses and assess the damage. And if we have been widowed or have experienced a traumatic breakdown, we also will need to assess our losses.

I was taken aback by how much I lost when my marriage ended and how much it affected me. It was not only the loss of my relationship with my husband, the person I talked to and with whom I shared my life, the good times and bad, but I lost the family structure I was so used to. I loved having my children with me all the time and now I had to share them with their father during the holidays. My son went to his dad's every other weekend and both children chose to live with him for a while at different times during their teenage years. It was a massive shock for me, and I had to learn how to parent from a distance. As my ex-husband was the main breadwinner at the time, I lost my income – only weeks before we separated, having no idea at all what was about to happen, I had given up my job to return to university to study. I also lost the relationships I had with most of my husband's family. And I lost all control of what was happening in my life.

I felt like I had lost my family and ruined everyone's lives.

MARK

When I present events for single parents, I often use the Jenga game as a way of illustrating the losses we incur at the initial stages of our journey. Carefully building the tower of wooden blocks, I explain that each block represents different aspects of the life we have built over the years: our house or home, our family relationships, our finances, our traditions, our identity, our children, our possessions, our friends, our marriage/couple relationship. And then I knock the tower down to depict what happens when the earthquake of separation, divorce or bereavement demolishes the components of our lives.

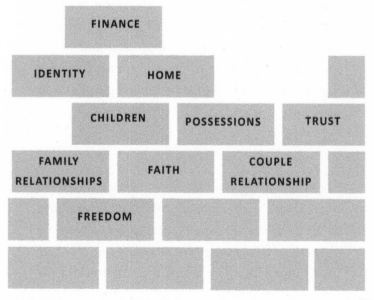

Next, looking at the rubble, I begin to pick the bricks up one at a time and start the process of rebuilding the wall. I tell the audience that constructing the wall will be a slower process this time; they will be doing it on their own and against a backdrop of heartache and pain. And that's why I want to stress once more how important it is to be gentle with and to pace ourselves at this stage of the journey – we have to build our wall one brick at a time rather than expect it to be finished overnight. The good news in all of this, however, is that we *can* rebuild it. It may take time and hard work, but we *will* be happy again.

Loss of intimacy and companionship

I miss having someone to talk to and share things with, as well as the intimacy that marriage brought me. We all have tough days and need that hug. I can come through my front door after a busy day (never mind tough!) and there's nobody there to care, or so it seems.

VAL

I miss not being able to share worries (even the silly things) with someone and sharing the joys as well. There are moments when something happens – like seeing the absolute joy on your child's face when they watch Bob the Builder *for the first time – and it's so hard having no one to share those moments.*

AMANDA

It may sound obvious, but when we lose a partner, we lose a companion – someone to talk to, someone who is there for us when times are good and when they are hard. I'd been with my husband for fifteen years and we'd shared everything together, so there was a huge empty void in my life when we broke up. I remember the first night alone, lying in that big bed all by myself. There was no one to roll over and say goodnight to or to chat to about something that was on my mind. Those early days felt extremely empty as I readjusted to a new way of life, and there's no getting away from it: it was extremely painful. For all of us in this situation, because we have lost the intimacy that we once had with our partner, it is vital that we seek and accept companionship and support from others, especially close and trusted friends and family and other single parents who have gone before us.

A word of warning: don't look for companionship in the wrong places, or seek a new romantic or sexual relationship too soon. Our basic emotional needs at this time are for security, acceptance, and healing – for people who will walk with us as we heal.

Loss of home and possessions

....

I had to sell the family home and move out of the town we lived in quite quickly, which also meant I lost my childminder and the children had to start a new school and make new friends.

CELIA

....

We spent the next five years going from one relative or friend's house to the next. I prayed earnestly for a home of our own. On many occasions, we had no food, water or decent clothing. Eventually, we had a flat to live in, but it was empty. We lived with just a mattress on the floor until I was able to buy simple furniture.

KATIE

....

I had to move back in with my mother. We became poor, almost overnight, as we had to leave our home suddenly, taking almost nothing with us.

SAMANTHA

Many of us will lose our home when we become single parents, perhaps because we've had a joint mortgage and need to sell the house to split the proceeds. If we are separated or divorced, we can also lose possessions – a wedding present, a photo album, a painting by a family member, or even the family pet. Deciding who keeps what can be problematic and there's no easy way of going about it. Be as fair as possible and do your utmost to keep your self-control during the process. You *can* get through it, even if the outcome seems unfair, and if you can do so with a little integrity, all the better. It may be helpful to have a third party come into the discussions to help you both find a happy medium and come to a final decision.

Loss of income

My husband and I both worked during our marriage. I went from having a part-time job as a district nurse and being financially comfortable to receiving income support and having to watch my money carefully.

HARRIET

Having less money was very testing. We had two adults bringing in two good wages, holidays in France and a new car. Afterwards, we had no holidays, no car, and a difficult last week of the month when money was very limited.

JACK

I was talking to one single-parent mum recently about money and she said, "Yeah – there is none." In fact, in the conversations I have with single parents, the loss of or lack of money is a recurring topic of conversation. If our partner was the main breadwinner, as mine was, our bereavement or the end of our relationship may mean that we have to find a job or claim benefits. If we have a home and a good job that pays the bills and gives us a little extra, we must count our blessings, because there can be serious hardship for some, especially if it's not possible for them to find a job, or a job that will fit around them caring for their children.

Loss of family and friends

I was very sad that my husband forbade his family to keep in contact with us. I felt I'd lost grandparents, cousins, and lovely in-laws.

ANGIE

I'd expected to lose some friends, but I was shocked that it was almost all of them. I came to the conclusion that the only way forward was to accept that they weren't real friends if they could abandon me at this hard time in my life. But it's very isolating and lonely.

BECKY

There's a saying that blood is thicker than water, and although it's not always the case, after a separation or divorce this is often shown to be true. When my marriage broke up, the majority of my ex-husband's family dissociated themselves from me. I had no family support in the UK, so you can imagine that it wasn't an easy situation for me. I soon realized that the important thing was to build up relationships with others who would support me.

During a separation or divorce, friends are in a difficult position; they have a choice as to whether to try to support both parties (not easy in practical terms) or to take sides. It can be a shock and terribly hurtful, but if our mutual friends choose not to support us, we have two options: to be offended and let the hurt fester inside us or to move on so that we don't suffer further heartache and pain. I know this is much easier said than done, but in time we can start to make new friends and build a different friendship network. This was what helped me to distance myself from my ex-husband and create a new life for myself.

Loss of status

I am a district nurse/midwife and I bumped into one of the mums I'd had at my antenatal classes. She treated me differently when she realized that I now lived in a council house in a rough area as opposed to the privately owned house in the country that was my home before my divorce.

KELLY

I had to move in with my mother. I was a burden and then a thing of mockery, and I was treated as such.

ESME

I felt I had become a stereotype (black, single mother) and was looked down upon. And I felt I'd lost status in the eyes of my church, some family, and friends. I was told that other women looked on me as a threat because, potentially, I could prey on their partners. I noticed that I couldn't have conversations with men of my own age group who were married. I felt that I had become a second-class citizen.

DARLA

I felt I lost status and honour (respectability) by no longer being a married parent. However, I also lost the abuse, which is a good thing!

LILAH

Many single parents feel that people's attitude towards them changes and that even their family and friends treat them differently from before. There can be a stigma attached to our status. I remember feeling that I had to continually justify or explain why I was a single parent. I believe the only way to battle misconceptions is to change society's attitude. Single parents are some of the strongest and hardest working individuals I have ever met, and by telling our story, we can inform others and give them more understanding and insight.

Loss of freedom

I lost freedom and personal space. I couldn't go out on my own as there was no one to look after the children any more. My children were so distressed by the divorce that they slept with me for years afterwards.

SHANA

For single parents, particularly those with younger children, loss of freedom is a huge issue. If we are co-parenting with our ex-partner, with some negotiation and planning it may be possible to arrange childcare with them so that we can pop out to the shops, go to an exercise class, go for a quick pint with a mate, or visit the dentist without too much hassle.

Loss of hopes and dreams

My dreams of retiring, travelling, and sharing my future with my husband were dashed.

JOAN

....

*I felt grief and loss: loss of the hope and beliefs of
what our future would be and, I suppose, a grief for
the desire I had to be in a "complete" family. This
feeling seems to be going on a long time. I have been
divorced for four years now and I still feel sad.*

JANE

Whether our hopes and dreams for the future were out
in the open or unspoken, we will all have had them –
hopes or ambitions for our children, dreams of having
grandchildren, aspirations to undertake new activities
with our partner, or plans for our retirement. Many of
those are now lost, and everything can seem hopeless, but
the single-parent journey is all about change. We can still
have hopes and dreams, but they will be new ones. There
came a point in my journey when I did feel able to dare to
dream again and from then on I started to thrive – to build
a new life. That time will come for you too.

Chapter 4

GRIEF

....

When my wife Joanne died suddenly at the age of forty-eight, the shock that hit me at first was as if a sledgehammer had been taken to my emotions. After that, the numbness kicked in. The overwhelming sadness and heartache as I mourned for her is hard to describe – it was like a cloud that enveloped me. I yearned for my wife who was no longer here. The absence of her presence was powerful and painful. Trying to cope with this and still somehow function with everyday tasks that could not be ignored was very difficult for me.

STEVE

It felt like grief – surprisingly. I lost my appetite and wanted to withdraw from all social contact, even things like Facebook. It felt very scary and overwhelming. I had to deal with so much stuff – looking for somewhere to live, claiming benefits, finding work, and coping with normal day-to-day stress. I felt like my head was constantly buzzing.

ANNA

I grieved. I was suffering the loss of my hopes, dreams, and plans. My life had suddenly headed off in a different direction. That is incredibly hard when it's not what you have chosen – when it's a result of someone else's decision.

SAMMIE

One of the definitions of grief is "keen mental suffering or distress over affliction or loss" and it is most commonly associated with bereavement. Many of those who are divorced experience grief for the loss of their marriage. These feelings will usually be more intense at the beginning, and there's no fixed time for how long they will last. Sadness, yearning, anxiety, panic, anger, guilt, and confusion can all be experienced in waves and may return at unpredictable times.

In the first months after my marriage ended, there was an intensity of grief and pain far greater than I'd ever had before. I remember that I read another single parent's description of her experience, and it perfectly captured how I felt: "I felt despair. I thought I was dying. I didn't believe anyone could feel so much emotional pain and still be alive. I felt hopeless, helpless, worthless and abandoned."[3]

The grief process

> *Grief is as unique as you are, and as individual as a fingerprint. Each person will be affected in his or her own way because everyone is different – even in the same family.*[4]

There are no set rules or a specific sequence of neat stages in the grief process, no right or wrong way to cope, and no one set of emotions to feel. Sometimes grief is at its most intense at the initial time of loss and sometimes the intensity will be felt later. We may feel on top of our emotions one minute, but be completely overwhelmed by them the next, and we may go through that cycle several times in the same day! Paediatrician Dr Richard Wilson has likened this to being caught up in a whirlpool: we swirl round and round revisiting emotions until, at some point, the river catches us up and takes us in a different direction.[5]

---

3   Worth, J. and Tufnell, C., *Journey Through Single Parenting – A Practical Guide to Finding Fulfilment* (London: Hodder & Stoughton, 1997), p. 9.
4   *Help is at Hand: Support After Someone May Have Died Through Suicide* (Public Health England and the National Suicide Prevention Alliance, September 2015), p. 4.
5   Ward, B. et al, *Good Grief 2: Exploring Feelings, Loss and Death with Over Elevens and Adults* (London: Jessica Kingsley Publishers; 2nd revised edition, 1995), pp. 112–13.

Sometimes people who are close to us have their own opinions about how we should be feeling or what we should be doing. Even though this may be well meaning, it's important to allow ourselves to feel what we are feeling and only do what we are able to do. One young widower told me that his neighbour thought he'd grieved enough and urged him to go out and buy a new car to make himself feel better. He went along with it, but knew that it wouldn't help – he was still grieving and nowhere near able to start rebuilding his life. We need to listen to and be gentle with ourselves so that we can grieve and heal at our own pace.

Grief following bereavement

I wonder about when and how the dominoes had started to fall down and what actions might have stopped setting them into motion. I turn over in my mind what would have happened if we hadn't moved house, if I hadn't left my job, if we hadn't gone on holiday two months before she died, if I had given her more attention, or more space, said more, said less...[6]

After the death of a loved one, as well as grief, loss, and hopelessness it's not unusual for people to be angry or even to feel guilty. We may experience "survivor's guilt", especially

6   *Help is at Hand: Support After Someone May Have Died Through Suicide* (Public Health England and the National Suicide Prevention Alliance, September 2015), p. 4.

if we have escaped a tragic accident. After a suicide, the emotions we can feel have been described as "grief with the volume turned up".[7] We may feel bitter towards our partner or try to find someone to blame for their death; or we may feel guilty, wondering whether we could have prevented the suicide by doing or saying something differently. If our partner has died from an illness, we may blame the health professionals who were treating them for not doing more.

Psychologists suggest that an important factor in recovery is to develop healthy "continuing bonds" with the person we have lost.[8] This means that rather than letting go of our partner, we embrace the memories we have of them and the experiences we shared, speak of and about them, and incorporate their influence and memory into our future.

Sometimes, however, continuing those bonds may prove difficult for friends and family to accept. Kate Osher wrote about her experience:

So many people expect widows and widowers to forget. To move on. To stop talking about them. To pretend those chapters of our life didn't ever exist. The ghost makes so many people uncomfortable. I had men I was dating in the years after tell me "not to mention" my marriage or my husband's death to friends or family . . . I refused. Any of it. All of it. It's tricky, of course. It

---

7   Ibid.
8   Klass, D. et al (eds), *Continuing Bonds: New Understandings of Grief* (London: Routledge, 1996).

makes people uncomfortable sometimes. I'm remarried now to a man who never once has asked me to forget about my past. Never once told me my late husband needs to be excised from my life. It takes a special person to be open to being with someone who has loved and lost at such a deep level. I know that. And I try to be as respectful as I can be – but I can't pretend my life before did not exist. I can't pretend I don't think about my late husband. A lot. . .[9]

A key thing to bear in mind is that we can experience setbacks with grief even years down the road. In some ways, grief never really ends, but we *can* learn to live with it – we can find "a new normal". Many people find bereavement counselling very helpful, and I would encourage you to consider this if you are struggling. You might also like to get in touch with a specialist organization such as Care for the Family's Widowed Young Support. The team offer support through a telephone befriending service, newsletter, and special day and weekend events. Often people who attend speak of their relief at being able to talk with others who have experienced their specific loss and know just how hard it is to "move on".

---

9   Osher, K., "The Misunderstood Grief of a Person Whose Spouse Died by Suicide", The Mighty (19 January 2017). https://themighty.com/2017/01/spouse-partner-suicide-grief/

I am so glad I went on that weekend away for those who have been widowed young. I arrived without hope, and I left with bagfuls of it. I made fabulous friends who totally get what I am going through.

HEIDI

Grief following separation or divorce

Continuing bonds with the person we have lost is good advice for those who are bereaved, but when our relationship has broken down, we should do the opposite. We need to completely let go of our couple relationship and learn to interact with our ex-partner in a new way. And for our children's well-being, we should aim to have as positive a relationship with them as possible.

The process of formalizing a divorce or separation can be like repeatedly re-opening a wound. Perhaps we are co-parenting with our ex-partner and the interaction with them week after week when collecting or dropping off the kids opens us up to hurt again. We may find it painful to see them moving on with their life or having a new relationship. And if our ex-partner was responsible for the break-up or left us against our wishes, we can feel a deep sense of rejection. Denial and false hope can also be an issue for us – the hope of a reconciliation, the "what ifs", and the wish that things could go back to the way they were only bringing torment and uncertainty. Our memories of happier times in our relationship can produce very mixed emotions of loss and regret and, in some circumstances, they are tainted by the more recent memories of what has led to its breakdown.

The rawness and intense feelings will diminish over time, although they may never leave us completely. In the beginning, I thought about my loss and grieved deeply every day; I woke up thinking about it and fell asleep thinking about it. But after about a year, I suddenly realized it wasn't at the forefront of my mind, and my grief was not as intense. Now, although certain smells or places bring back memories, most of the time I don't feel the heartache that I did at the beginning.

If you feel you are struggling with grief and unable to move forward, consider seeking help from an experienced counsellor, who can gently support you as you take the next steps of your journey.

Healing does come. It will take longer for some of us than for others, but those intense feelings of grief *will* subside in the future.

Chapter 5

EMOTIONAL AFTERSHOCKS

If the life-changing process of becoming a single parent is a metaphorical earthquake in our lives, we should be prepared for some aftershocks in the form of emotional fall-out. This can include anger, self-pity, guilt, fear, and a sense of rejection or failure; it can hit immediately afterwards, or days, weeks, and even months later. In addition to the symptoms of emotional shock that we felt at first, we may experience heightened anxiety or fear, irritability, restlessness, sadness, depression, a sense of alienation, emotional outbursts, and confusion. We may make poor decisions, have memory problems, or become introverted and quiet, and some people can have recurring thoughts or dreams. It's not great reading, is it? But if you experience one or more of these aftershocks, please be assured that you are not going crazy and it's not just you!

Rather than trying to ignore emotions like these, it's important to acknowledge them, recognize that you are vulnerable, and be kind to yourself. When you can, try to get plenty of rest (not easy for single parents!) Accept any help offered to you – perhaps a friend or family member who will have the children for you now and again.

Anger and bitterness

I was angry at the reaction from people I trusted.

CHRISTY

I was overwhelmed and angry about how my husband treated me after he left.

JADE

I got angry at times and this is so not like me.

ALEX

One of the strongest human emotions is anger, and it's not hard to understand why it's a common experience of single parents. We may be angry at the way our ex-partner or others have treated us, and if we are bereaved we can even feel angry with our partner for leaving us behind to cope with raising a family alone. If we are co-parenting in difficult circumstances, perhaps with a person who can't be bothered or knows just how to push our buttons, we may have to cope with anger on a daily basis.

The danger is that if anger and bitterness remain unresolved they can get out of hand, affecting our attitudes, perceptions and relationships, and eventually destroying our lives. Signs of unresolved anger include jealousy, grudge-holding, harshness, sarcasm, resentfulness, coldness, judgmentalism, attention-seeking, and negativity – seeing the world in a bad light and every situation becoming an annoyance.

It's worth working hard at becoming self-aware so that we can recognize when we are angry and then express it safely and productively. Anger can come out through violence and aggression, both verbal and physical, so we must be careful about how our anger affects those around us. Have you ever found that you're shrieking at the children even though they haven't really done much at all – you've just snapped? But it's just as bad to bottle anger up; it will certainly come out at some stage, probably in a negative, uncontrolled way.

It's also important to be honest with others about how we are feeling, and at appropriate times that may even include letting our children know that we feel angry. It doesn't mean telling them *all* the details, but we can let them know that something has upset us and we are working through it. If we deal with anger in the right way, we set our children a great example for handling it in their own lives.

Anger is a call to action, not something to hold on to. We may need to put a past wrong right, ensure that the wrong will not be repeated, or to forgive it.

When I was angry, I would go into the garden and work there. It helped me to let go of my emotions and I always felt better afterwards.

LAURA

....

I put up a punching bag in my shed and go out there when the kids are in bed if I've had a bad day and need to let off some steam.

ROB

....

I write when I am angry or stressed. It helps when I can put things on paper.

TARA

Whether it's writing a journal, going for a run, walking the dog, going to the gym or doing some rigorous housework, it's a great idea to find a safe way of expressing anger. When my ex-husband had upset me, I used to go to bed and write a letter to him. I would pour my heart out, letting him know how I felt. In the morning, I would rip the letter up. I didn't need to send it to him. The purpose had been to release my feelings.

If you have a trusted friend or family member you can talk to, take advantage of them! They need to be someone who will allow you to get things off your chest without judging you. And although it may seem inappropriate, try to have some fun occasionally. I don't mean to be in any way dismissive of the circumstances that cause us to be angry, but laughter can be a great release and help to lighten the load. It can be as simple as watching a comedian on the TV after the children have gone to bed, or sharing a funny story with a friend.

Something that goes hand in hand with anger is forgiveness. When we can forgive others for the wrong they have done us, it releases the anger, bitterness, and hurt we're carrying inside and allows us to move forward. Forgiveness isn't easy – and many of us won't be anywhere near feeling that we want to forgive our ex-partner – but we'll take a look at this again in Part 4.

For the most part, the old saying that time heals is true. Whereas at the beginning of our journey we may be very angry, when we put more distance behind us, looking at things from a different perspective, we can find that our anger subsides. If your anger is not easing with time, or you feel that it's becoming uncontrollable and affecting not only yourself but those around you, do ask for professional help from your doctor. There's no shame in this; in fact, by seeking help you are taking positive action towards regaining control of your life.

Self-pity

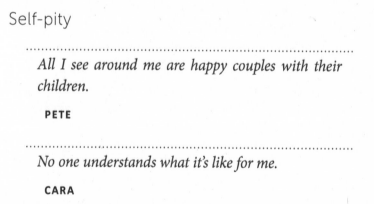

All I see around me are happy couples with their children.

PETE

No one understands what it's like for me.

CARA

Attacks of self-pity are common to everyone, and I for one can fully sympathize with the many single parents who have had a raw deal in life, whether it's through being abused or abandoned, or from being bereaved. But the truth is that if we stay in this mindset, it can lead to us having a "victim mentality" – we believe that we are always a victim and that bad things will always happen to us. This is debilitating and destructive; it steals our joy and we don't see the bigger picture of the good things in life that we *do* have.

> *Self-pity is easily the most destructive of the non-*
> *pharmaceutical narcotics; it is addictive, gives*
> *momentary pleasure and separates the victim from*
> *reality.*
>
> **JOHN W. GARDNER**

Psychologist Andrea Mathews says that someone with a victim mentality will be telling themselves things like, "Don't get up, as you'll only get kicked down again", "My life is really, really hard", and "You can't trust anyone." She explains that these beliefs protect the person from "ever having to really engage life and hurdle its hurdles. Doing so is just plain too risky. No, the best way to cope is to just stay on the down-side of life, and never, never, never expect more."[10]

---

10   Mathews, A., "The Victim Identity: The allergic reaction to personal responsibility means a difficult life", *Psychology Today* (24 February 2011). www.psychologytoday.com/gb/blog/traversing-the-inner-terrain/201102/the-victim-identity

To combat self-pity, I found it helped to think intentionally about the things in my life that were good. A friend gave me a "thankful journal" for my birthday, and writing in it each day made me stop and identify the things I was grateful for: my children, my health, a kind word from a friend. We may not have chosen to be treated badly or to have suffered in the way we have; however, we *can* choose how we deal with it and how we move forward.

....

What helped me was when I found that, even in the worst moment, it was possible to find something to be thankful for.

TRACY

Guilt

For a long time I felt very guilty that my children were now in the category of "coming from a single-parent home", and I've discovered that many single parents carry a burden of guilt of some sort. We may feel guilty that we stayed in an abusive relationship for as long as we did and that our children saw way more than they should have done. Perhaps we feel uncomfortable about how much time we have to spend away from our kids, even if it is because we need to work to provide for them. We may blame ourselves for not being able to give our children the things they want, for having to move to a different area or live in a smaller house. And we may feel guilty about our past choices or actions: "Why did

I ever get together with him/her in the first place?" or "Did I try hard enough to keep our relationship together?" If we're not careful, we can find ourselves constantly regretting and going over the past. I've been there myself. Many times I daydreamed my afternoon away, wondering if I could have done something different.

> *Years later, I felt guilt about my actions, what I had put my ex through, and I realized it was my fault.*
>
> **JOHN**

> *I felt guilty becoming a single parent. I was embarrassed and depressed about how I was going to cope and succeed on my own.*
>
> **LAURA**

> *I felt so guilty. Why didn't I separate from my kids' father earlier? But, on the other hand, was I depriving them of a father, even though the situation was dire and at times dangerous?*
>
> **JOANNE**

To move forward on our journey, we have to release ourselves from guilt. This means that if we have been at fault, whether fully or partially, rather than trying to justify or rationalize our actions, we need to take responsibility for them. When we do this, and try to make amends wherever possible, we can more easily accept the past, learn from it, and put it behind us.

We may be feeling another kind of guilt – false guilt. This is where we blame ourselves inappropriately: "I work such long hours. Perhaps if I'd been at home more often, she wouldn't have looked for someone else" or "I put on so much weight this year. Perhaps, if I'd done something about it, he wouldn't have left me for another woman." And other people, perhaps our ex-partner, may lay those same false accusations against us: "If you hadn't been away so much. . ." or "If you'd taken care of yourself a bit more. . ."

We can even have guilty feelings about the death of our partner because of accusations we make against ourselves or even those that others make against us: "Should I have made her/him get that lump checked out sooner?" or "Why didn't I drive on the night of the car accident? I should have known he/she was really tired."

It's important to address inappropriate guilt and find out where it originated. It is not ours to own and we need to give ourselves permission to be released from it.

Embarrassment and rejection

....

I was embarrassed and found it difficult to talk to anyone about it – the school, work, even utility companies.

SARAH

....

I just sat at home watching TV, all day, every day. It was how I coped. I didn't want to put myself out there any more to get hurt.

GILL

....

I felt so alone and rejected when my ex walked out. It was especially painful as I later found out that she'd been seeing another man whilst she was still living with me. I couldn't understand what he had to offer her that I didn't and how she could just up and leave us all.

BEN

Many of us experience rejection at the beginning of our journey, especially if we were left by our partner. The person we loved the most has made us feel that we're no good; they don't want us, don't need us, and they're not going to be there for us any more. We can also feel rejected by family or friends, and we can feel judged by society for the break-up of our family, for not working and instead claiming benefits, or for going to work and putting our children into childcare.

Different people react to rejection in different ways. Some of us may appear to be coping well on the surface but won't allow people to become too emotionally close – we put up barriers to try to protect ourselves. Others of us may be desperate to prove ourselves worthy of being loved, and perhaps smother everyone around with inappropriate affection (with the result that they run for the hills!)

If we are struggling with feelings of rejection we need to face them head on in order to be healed from them. I've said it many times in this book, but trusted friends and family can play a big part in helping us. Remember, too, that not everyone will treat us in the same way.

Fear

Initially, I felt really fearful that I couldn't do it.

BRENDAN

I was concerned for my children's and my own future. I was afraid I wouldn't be able to cope emotionally, as well as practically and financially. I had to keep on going for my sons' sakes.

MIA

I was terrified, as I had no support network whatsoever. I was living in a hostel in a rough area and holding down a full-time job, the wages of which went to pay hostel and childminding fees. I had to allow myself "time off" from worry, as it was hard to function. My escapism was reading each night before I went to sleep.

KAREN

Fear is another one of the big emotional aftershocks that affect single parents. We can be fearful about our ability to keep a roof over our heads and provide for our children; we can have a generalized, overwhelming fear of the future; and we can be afraid that we are failing as a parent. Like other emotions we have discussed, fear is debilitating and crippling.

One of the keys to dealing with fears is to distinguish between those we can do something about and those outside of our control. One of my greatest fears concerned who would look after my children if I became ill or went into hospital. After a while, I realized there was something I could do to address it. I made a list of friends who were happy to be contacted at any time in an emergency, and put their phone numbers on my fridge door. I also spoke to my ex-husband about how he could be contacted in an emergency. Although I couldn't do anything to prevent the possibility of that emergency ever happening, the big fear of what would happen to the children was taken care of.

Even with fears about things outside our control, what we do have control of is our *attitude* to them. We can say to ourselves, "Yes, I am afraid about. . . but I am not going to let it get the better of me." I remember a mum on one of our single-parent family holidays saying, "Kat, I can't wait to go home!" I felt so worried. I said, "Really? Has the holiday been that bad?" "No, Kat," she replied. "It has been that *good*! Today I overcame my fear of heights when I went down the zip wire. I now know that if I can do this, I can do so much more when I get home. I can deal with other fears that are holding me back."

As we get further along in our journey we'll find that we are stronger than we ever imagined. We have faced the giants of fear in our lives and lived to tell the tale.

Part 2

The parenting highway: raising our children

Chapter 1

IS IT BECAUSE I'M A SINGLE PARENT?

I remember sitting in a café with a group of friends. We were enjoying a coffee and catching up with each other. A single mother we knew came in with her toddler, and he was having a massive tantrum. She did the best she could with ordering, paying, and transporting her coffee and cake to a nearby table while her son continued to scream and cry. One of my friends turned to the rest of us, rolled her eyes, and commented, "It's because she's a single parent." I couldn't believe what she'd said. That little boy wasn't having a tantrum because his mother was a single parent; he was having a tantrum because that's what kids do at times. My son had one tantrum in his whole childhood while we were out shopping (yes, I was fortunate!) and it was when my ex-husband and I were still married.

Many of us are plagued with guilt about behaviour problems we experience with our kids, thinking they are due to them being brought up in a single-parent home; however, the fact is that all children can be challenging at times. The issues we experience with our kids are often exactly the same as those experienced by *all* parents – not just because we're single parents.

But that's not to say that the task of parenting is the same for single parents as for those in a relationship. Parenting is hard at times, and it's especially hard when you're doing it alone.

....

I was so frightened that I would not cope with bringing the children up correctly, or even that I was capable of actually bringing them up.

JENNA

You're not alone

At Care for the Family we believe that people often struggle with the terrible feeling that "It's just me". Whether it's a crisis in our relationship, a challenging issue with our teenagers, or the sheer exhaustion of coping with small children, we can feel totally isolated. But the truth is that we're not alone. That fact dawned on me when I read a book on single parenting for the first time. I realized just how many people out there were dealing with the same issues as myself. That revelation made an incredible difference to me. What I was going through was awful, but it was totally normal and I felt a huge relief. It gave me a glimmer of hope that at some point things would get better.

Some of us may feel as though we're the worst ever mum or dad – especially at tea time when chaos rules, the children are tired and hungry, *we're* tired and hungry, and we still have a meal to prepare and bath time and bedtime to get through. When my children were at primary school, the time when my stress levels hit their peak was first thing on a weekday morning when getting the children ready for the school run. In the midst of brushing hair, finding PE kit, looking for book bags, preparing lunch boxes, and finding missing shoes, I remember the sheer frustration and exhaustion of trying to get two children with no concept of time ready to leave the house. In my mind's eye, I could see their teacher waiting for us to arrive and tutting that we were late again.

And then, when we'd beaten all the odds and actually arrived at the school gates, all the other parents seemed so cool, calm, and collected. I felt totally incompetent. Why couldn't I take mornings in my stride like they did? One day I decided to talk about how I felt with a few close friends who were parents. And surprise! I wasn't the only one struggling with the early morning school run.

Children can be compliant, testing or a mixture of both. Compliant children do as they are told, obey the rules, and are generally easy-going, going with the flow. Children who are testing, on the other hand, test boundaries often, are difficult, self-opinionated, and dig their heels in. If you are the parent of a compliant child, it is vital that you don't judge those who have testing ones. Make sure at all costs that you don't start to hand out advice to others about how they should parent. In no way is this helpful. And be especially wary if there's any chance you might have more children one day, because you may well have a testing child who is sent to you to blow your previous parenting experience out of the water!

It's common for parents with more than one child to discover that their children are like chalk and cheese – that was certainly the case with my own. I've often heard a parent talk about one of their offspring being feisty, self-opinionated, and having attitude, whereas the other is laid-back, easy-going, and usually does as they are told.

All parents struggle with challenging parenting issues at one time or another, whether or not they are single, and somehow we just have to get our kids through it and out the other side. My children are now young adults and I have a great relationship with them and am very proud of them both.

Generation after generation of parents have dealt with testing children, but knowing this doesn't make it any easier. Raising teenagers was the hardest thing I ever had to do alone, but when I realized that the ups and downs I had with my children were the same as those experienced by parents the world over, it gave me a huge sense of relief. Whatever parenting issues you are facing, you may feel that it's just you, but I encourage you with all my heart to take hold of the truth that *you are not alone*.

Focus on the things that make a difference

Am I a good parent? Am I doing it right?

JONAH

Maybe as you read this book you are thinking, "I can't do this." Most parents will question their parenting skills at one time or another, but single parents do so even more. It's hard to know if you're doing a good job when you don't have anyone at home to encourage you or help you improve when you fall short.

We may worry about the effects on our children of growing up in a single-parent home. Will they be OK? Although there are concerning statistics about the outcomes for children in single-parent households, such outcomes are not inevitable. There are some key factors that positively influence children's well-being and these are things over which we do have control: the quality of the relationship between the parent and the child; the quality of parenting they receive; and the effect of a home environment that is warm, harmonious and peaceful.[11] So rather than doubting our abilities as parents and worrying about negative predictions for our children, we can focus our attention and energy on these important factors.

Having guilt-busting friends with whom we can chat, offload feelings and compare notes is very helpful. Not only does it help us see that we are not alone, but it will highlight when we are being too hard on ourselves – we'll realize that others make mistakes from time to time as well. Sharing our experiences also allows us to learn from and encourage each other. We're all human and no one is perfect; we're all just doing the best we can. Let's change perspective and start to

11   Pedro-Carroll, J., "How Parents Can Help Children Cope with Separation/Divorce", Encyclopedia on Early Childhood Development (June 2011).   www.child-encyclopedia.com/divorce-and-separation/according-experts/how-parents-can-help-children-cope-separationdivorce

tell ourselves the things we are doing *right*. If we've had an incredibly challenging day but have still managed to feed, clothe and clean our kids, get them to school and tuck them up in bed, well done to us!

Chapter 2

PARENTING STYLES

As parents, our goal for our children is to nurture them physically, emotionally, and spiritually. We'll aim to ensure they are kept warm and fed, feel loved, accepted and safe, and that they enjoy their childhood. And we'll help to prepare them for adult life, build their resilience to cope with setbacks, and encourage them to make good relationships and add something to society. But if we want to achieve these goals – and we do! – a key choice we need to make is *how* we parent.

Our particular style of parenting will drive how we actually carry out bringing up our children every day. Broadly speaking, there are three different parenting styles. The one we choose to adopt will be influenced by how we've been brought up ourselves, as well as by our individual values, temperament and personality. Let's take a closer look at the options.

Authoritarian parenting

Authoritarian parents will have lots of rules in their home and strict ideas about discipline and behaviour. They are not open to any discussion and like to be in control. Often, they are perfectionists. Children with an authoritarian parent may feel as if they are living in the military; the phrase "Do as you're told and don't argue" will probably be quite familiar.

The advantage of this style of parenting is that everyone is clear about what is and isn't allowed, but children can feel suffocated and be unable to learn or think independently. So, although parenting like this may look as if it's working when the children are younger, when they become teenagers they can be resentful and push back against the tight control.

Permissive parenting

The permissive style of parenting is almost the complete opposite of the authoritarian style. This parent is very relaxed and laid back about behaviour and discipline; they impose few rules, and even fewer consequences if those rules are broken. Some parents who have grown up under authoritarian parents may swing to this extreme as a reaction to their upbringing. A typical response from this parent might be: "Do whatever you want." Children raised by permissive parents may have the space to become independent, but a big danger is that they can feel their parents don't love them or don't care, and they can become fearful and insecure. Permissive parenting can also make our children believe that the world revolves around them; this fails to equip them for the reality of life in an adult world that does not stop when we don't get our way.

Assertive parenting

Parents with an assertive parenting style understand the need for boundaries for their child's safety and security; however, these boundaries are set in the context of a warm, healthy relationship. They make as few rules as possible and choose their battles. A key characteristic is that they are willing to explain and discuss rules for behaviour and adapt these at times, allowing negotiation on both sides, but keeping the boundaries very clear over the things that matter to them. So a conversation with this parent may go something like this: "Yes, you can do that if. . ." or "No, you can't do that because. . ." Children are given appropriate freedom within limits, which helps them learn that actions and choices have consequences. Experts say that assertive parenting is the style we should aim for.

Some matters of behaviour will be more important to us than others, so the key thing about being an assertive parent is to establish what is important for *us*.

Chapter 3

BOUNDARIES

Rules without relationships lead to rebellion.[12]

Giving our children boundaries is vital, not only to keep them safe and healthy but to teach them about acceptable behaviour, help them learn self-control and give them a sense of security. It's also important that the discipline we give is both loving and consistent.

Boundaries need to be age-appropriate and will change as our children grow up. They will include, for example, what time they go to bed or come home at night, how much screen time they have, and what we expect from them with regard to their speech and behaviour. Enforcing boundaries is not always easy for any parent (it's natural for kids to push against them), but it can be particularly difficult for single parents because, as with other aspects of parenting, we have to do it alone with no one to back us up.

---

12   McDowell, J., *Why True Love Waits: The definitive book on how to help your youth resist sexual pressure* (Illinois: Tyndale House Publishers, 2002), p. 203.

As single parents, we don't have the luxury of asking the other parent to help deal with the kids when they are sick or acting up; we are on call 24/7 and it can be exhausting. And when we're feeling exhausted it can be difficult to enforce the consequences of a crossed boundary. It's important not to be hard on ourselves when that happens. Practically, as long as the child is not in danger, it may be better to let the issue go for the time being and deal with it when we have sufficient energy to follow through with any consequences. Remember: we're not super-human and tomorrow is another day!

It can also be harder for us if our children have experienced pain or loss, as we may feel guilty about giving boundaries and enforcing consequences when these are crossed. Perhaps we think they have been through enough already and it would be kinder to ignore bad behaviour or let them off the hook when they break the rules. That's understandable, but the truth is that boundaries are *good* for children. They keep them safe, give them security and help them mature into responsible adults. If we always let them have their own way, when they are adults our kids can have the same expectations, and we all know how unrealistic that is in healthy relationships and the world of work.

If you are worried about whether or not you are being too hard on your child, it's helpful to turn to trusted friends for an unbiased and honest opinion.

Say what you mean and mean what you say

Saying what you mean and meaning what you say is a key principle for parents, especially when it comes to enforcing the boundaries. Children need consistent discipline – they need to know that when their parent says no, they mean no and will not give in, regardless of how much they whine or make a scene. As a single parent it can be difficult to be consistent when our resources are low and we have no one to back us up, but it will reap benefits in the long run.

We need to be gentle but firm when dealing with our children. Speaking in a wishy-washy tone gives them the impression that we're not concerned or that we aren't 100 per cent certain about our decision, fuelling the possibility that they could persuade us to change our mind. If they are used to us saying what we mean, they won't bother pestering us. When we *don't* mean what we say, we put our kids in the position of never knowing whether or not they can believe us.

Choose your battles

One of the most sensible parenting principles I've come across is to choose your battles. We need to stick to our guns over issues that we feel very strongly about, but it's also wise to give and take when we can. When my daughter was fourteen, she asked me if she could dye her hair blue. She must have seen how mortified I was because she added, "It's cool, Mum. Don't worry. I only want slices of blue in it." As if this was supposed to make me feel better! My immediate reaction was, "No way, honey!" However, the more I thought about it, the more I concluded that in the grand scheme of things, hair colour really wasn't such a big deal. It wasn't going to hurt her, she could grow it out or get it re-dyed back to her natural colour, and it may even look nice! I ended up letting her get it done. This didn't happen when she asked me if she could get her belly button pierced. I spoke to a body piercer, who advised against it at my daughter's age. She said that she'd seen so many girls have problems with piercings, including getting infections that can be extremely painful and can leave a permanent scar. In the light of that I decided to say no to my daughter and explained my reasons. It was one battle I was prepared to fight.

Putting a few structures and systems in place can help make single parenting that bit easier and, ultimately, more enjoyable. It may be tempting to let our children get away with more than they used to, but even though this sometimes feels kinder, it is actually the opposite of what they need. Clear, consistent boundaries will give them structure and security, and allow them to grow into mature, confident adults.

Chapter 4

FILL UP YOUR CHILD'S EMOTIONAL TANK

All human beings have some basic emotional needs: to feel loved, to belong, to feel that we are good at something and to feel good about ourselves. So how do we best fulfil those needs in our children? In *The 5 Love Languages of Children*,[13] Gary Chapman and Ross Campbell explain that every child has an "emotional tank" that you can fill up with love. And just as a car is fuelled by the petrol in its tank, if a child's emotional tank is full it will fuel them through the challenges of childhood and adolescence. As their parents, we will be the main people in our children's lives to keep that tank topped up. The following list is not exhaustive, but includes some of the key things we can do to meet their needs now and build a solid foundation for their emotional well-being in the future.

---

13   Chapman, G. D. and Campbell, R., *The 5 Love Languages of Children* (Chicago: Northfield Publishing, reissue edition 2012), p. 17.

Time and attention

Spending time with our children without interruption is far from easy as a single parent, but so important for children – and for us. I know we've heard it all before, but it's still easy to somehow fail to grasp the fact that our children won't stay young for ever. The years of childhood pass all too swiftly, and our fledglings will fly the nest before we know it, so we need to make the most of them.

Work commitments, caring for elderly relatives, and carrying out the never-ending tasks of shopping, cooking, and cleaning, will all affect the amount of time we can spend with our kids, but we can be intentional about seizing opportunities. Many parents find that meals around the table together, when you can all chat about how the day has gone, are important, but we can also do one-off things such as going out for day trips together or having pyjama days in. If finances are tight, having days out may not be an easy option, but we can still find fun, free things to do, such as going for a walk, having a picnic or watching movies at home.

A more recent phenomenon to be aware of is "distracted parenting". This is where parents are spending so much time on their smartphones – phone calls, emails, social media – that they simply don't give their full attention to their child. If this is an issue for us, we can take steps to break the habit now – for instance, by checking emails and using social media only after they are in bed.

If we have more than one child, it will be especially meaningful to give each of them some one-to-one time now and again. When my children were older, I found this easier with my daughter, as we had similar interests and would have girlie pamper nights or go out for coffee. However, I did find something to do one-to-one with my teenage son – playing pool! I am absolutely rubbish at it, but it was something fun we could do together. You can easily do a web search that will bring up hundreds of other ideas.

I remember trying my best to support my children through the initial stages of the break-up with my husband. They dealt with it very differently. My daughter was a young teenager who wanted to spend most of her time out with her friends, but my son was younger and spent most of his time with me. I was able to go with him back to my family in the US for a few weeks in the summer (my daughter chose not to accompany us on that occasion but came out with us the following year). That one-to-one time with my son was so important, as he was able to have space and start to heal from the hurt and turmoil he was in.

Not everyone will have the privilege of being able to get away like this, but if you can, look for any opportunity to have one-to-one time with each child. If you have family or friends who can look after your other children while you spend time with just one of them, do take advantage of this. If there is no one who can do this for you, consider rotating one-to-one time with each child every Friday night while the others watch a film on TV.

Unconditional love and acceptance

Giving our children unconditional love and acceptance is sometimes easier said than done. It doesn't mean that we approve of their every action all the time, but as Rob Parsons says:

> *We do our children a wonderful service if we send them into [the] world with an unshakeable belief that there is at least one person who, irrespective of their grades, weight or athletic genius, loves them – anyway. It really is the greatest gift. Most of us, as adults, are still searching for somebody to love us like that.*[14]

If our child's other parent has died or walked out on them, it's especially important to let them know that we are going to be there for them no matter what. We'll look at some practical aspects of showing our children love and affection in the section on "love languages".

Encouragement and support

Giving our children praise and encouragement is not about flattery, but an important way of affirming them when they do well. It can celebrate achievements and successes, no matter how small, and it can praise good behaviour such as being kind, generous or helpful. We can also make sure

---

14   Parsons, R., *The Sixty Minute Mother* (London: Hodder & Stoughton, 2009), p. 31.

that we come alongside our kids when they are discouraged, low or hurting to offer a listening ear and practical and emotional support.

Just as we want our children to treat us with respect, we can speak to them respectfully. How we talk and listen to our children greatly affects the quality of our relationship, and when we ask for and listen to their opinions it sends a message to them that we are considerate of and value them.

Filling our children's emotional tanks with unconditional love and affection is all about affirming and accepting them for who they are, not for what they do or don't do (although that doesn't mean we will always *like* them; when our teenager is being particularly obnoxious, we may feel the exact opposite!). For children who have experienced the death of a parent, divorce or relationship break-up, knowing that we love them unconditionally is especially important as it will help them deal with issues such as resentment, guilt, insecurity, rejection or fear.

Some children may choose not to accept love from one or both of their parents if they are feeling hurt or angry towards them. This can be very hurtful and frustrating, and may mean that we simply have to wait while making sure they know that our love for them is not conditional upon their love for us.

Regularly topping up our child's love tank when our own is running low can be difficult, so we shouldn't be afraid to get help to do that when we can. In fact, no parent can single-handedly meet a child's need for love, so wherever possible ask extended family, grandparents, aunts and uncles, close friends, and churches or other faith groups to play a role.

Don't wait for people to come up and ask you if they can help. If they have not experienced being part of a single-parent family, they may not know or understand what you are going through, or they may not want to step on your toes and interfere. Getting other adults involved in our children's lives is not always an easy thing to do, particularly if we're going through a period when we feel very isolated socially. However, it's well worth doing all we can to find that friend, relative, church/faith group or youth worker to invest in our child's life. Before we do that, though, it's essential that we know the person well, trust them completely, and are sure they will be a wise and helpful mentor for our child. We also need to be sensitive to our children and talk to them beforehand to ensure they are happy for that person to be involved.

Love languages

Although we all have the same need for love and affection, we have different ways of expressing and receiving this. It's therefore helpful for both us and our children if we can identify how they best understand love. Many people have found the principles outlined in *The 5 Love Languages of Children* extremely helpful.[15] In their book, the authors explain that the "love languages" are different ways of giving and receiving love, and we all have one or two of these as our primary love language.

---

15   Chapman, G.D. and Campbell, R., *The 5 Love Languages of Children* (Chicago: Northfield Publishing, reissue edition 2012), p. 17.

The five languages they identify are:

• *Words of affirmation.* Praise and encouragement is particularly meaningful for children with this primary love language. It is not just about praising their achievement and behaviour but about appreciating them for the unique and special person they are.

• *Quality time.* Children may understand love in this way if they like you giving them your undivided attention – watching them while they're playing, taking them out shopping or going for a coffee, for example. If they have brothers or sisters, when you can, try to create some one-to-one alone time with them.

• *Receiving gifts.* For children with this love language, gifts are a tangible sign of love. It's not about the cost and the size of the present – it could be a bar of chocolate or a pack of felt tips, a bunch of wild flowers or a pretty stone. Recognizing that they prefer this to a hug is an important step in communicating our love to them.

• *Acts of service.* We are doing acts of service for our children all the time, of course, but a child who has this as their primary love language will feel especially loved when you do things that are particularly important to them – for example, helping them with homework or giving a teenager a lift instead of them having to catch the bus.

• *Physical touch.* Babies need to be held and cuddled, and as children grow up, many still understand love through physical affection. For a child with this love language, things like a hug, a cuddle as you are watching TV together on the sofa, or a simple touch on the arm are especially important.

Learning to speak our child's love language can take time, but if we are patient and make the effort, it will bring a depth and closeness to our relationship that we may never have thought possible.

Chapter 5

HELPING OUR CHILDREN THROUGH SEPARATION, DIVORCE, AND BEREAVEMENT

Like adults, children will cope with grief in different ways and experience the emotions of grief at different times. Some may be angry and others may be in denial. Some may refuse to talk about what has happened, perhaps becoming introverted or withdrawn, and others may exhibit their feelings by throwing tantrums or being destructive. Whether it is buried or on the surface, they will experience grief, shock, and loss, although in a different way from us.

Bereaved children will re-visit the emotions of grief at different stages of their lives and this will be linked to their development. For example, young children move in and out of grief very quickly, one moment sobbing and a short while later running around laughing. We should also be prepared for significant events in life – Christmas plays, receiving awards, exam results, proms, going to university, marriage – to potentially cause distress and perhaps setbacks.

Children who continue to see our ex-partner when our relationship has ended may sometimes feel they can't talk about him or her. Perhaps they are afraid of upsetting us or feel that we would disapprove or be angry. Although it can be hard to hear, it's important that we allow them to talk about what they've been doing with their other parent if they want to, although we should never grill them about this. We also need to let them feel free to talk about memories of times they had with him or her in the past.

It will take time for them to heal, just as it does with us, so be patient and be there for them no matter what. Stability, consistent discipline, familiar routines, and unconditional love are more important than ever at this time. If, over time, your child continues to exhibit severe emotional distress, it may be helpful to seek professional help for them.

Emotions our children may go through

Anger and denial

As we have seen, a common response to grief is anger, and in children this may be directed at both parents, the parent who died or left the relationship, God or other people. While some children can withdraw and not let their feelings out, others can become angry and aggressive, physically destructive or arrogant.

My children each dealt with it very differently when their father left me. My daughter bottled up her emotions and didn't like to talk about the situation at all, whereas my gentle, laid-back son became angry and aggressive –

which upset him further and made him feel guilty. One day, he asked me why he was like it, so I told him that he had good cause to feel angry – it was normal and it wasn't wrong. Rather than expecting our kids to keep a lid on their emotions, we can help them to express these safely. I bought my son a punching bag and enrolled him in Judo lessons, which he loved. Be especially prepared for anger in younger children to come out in their behaviour, as they will not have the language to communicate it verbally. Drawing pictures, writing a journal, composing a song or taking dance or drama classes are all good ways of expressing emotions. After a bout of anger or aggression, let your child calm down and try to talk with them about what triggered it and how it made them feel. Let them know that your love for them does not depend on them being perfectly behaved all the time – you love them unconditionally.

Many children whose parents' relationship has ended will live in denial, perhaps fantasizing about them getting back together and even working towards making that happen. Sometimes this can continue for years afterwards, even if one of the parents has remarried. As hard as it is, we should be honest with our children about our relationship, rather than give in to the temptation to give them false hope.

Feeling out of control

Children can also feel completely powerless, because they cannot do anything about what has happened. To help them regain a sense of having some control, we can give them choices. For younger children it might be asking them what colour jumper they want to wear, or whether they want chips or boiled potatoes for tea, and for older children it might be asking them to choose from a list of things to do at half-term or a shortlist of places to go on holiday. Asking for their thoughts and opinions on things will also help them to feel valued.

Fear and rejection

Our children may feel unloved or rejected if their other parent has left the family, even if he or she tells them otherwise. And they may develop the fear that we too will reject them. We can tell them something along the lines of: "Daddy left because he doesn't love Mummy any more, but he still loves you." However, this doesn't stop them thinking: "If Daddy once loved Mummy but doesn't any more, will he stop loving me too?" They may be confused that a parent could love them but still leave them, and they may even conclude that their parents are lying to them. We will need to constantly reassure them about how much we love them, and try to explain that this love won't change.

Some children may be clingy because they are fearful that as their other parent has left, we may do so too. They may be worried about the future: "Will I ever see Daddy/ Mummy again?", "Now that Daddy has died, who will chat to me about football and take me to watch the match?", "Will I still be able to live here or will we have to move?", "Will we have enough money?" or "Will Mum/Dad cope on their own?" Communication is key here because the more we understand our children's fears, the more we will be able to give them reassurance.

For children whose parent has chosen to cut off all contact with them, the feelings of loss, guilt, rejection and unworthiness can be even greater. They may assume that it is their fault, that they deserved to be abandoned, or that their parent is better off without them. It's important to explain to them that this is not the case and to reassure them of our unconditional love. We can also take every opportunity to build their self-esteem by praising them and telling them how proud we are of them, and we can enlist other adults who are close to our children to give them encouragement and positive feedback about their character, talents and abilities.

Some children choose to reject the absent parent altogether and others idealize them or have fantasy memories about them to help them cope with their hurt. If your child is really struggling with these issues, it might be helpful to talk to your local GP about counselling.

Guilt

Some children can feel guilty about their parents' divorce, separation or death: "If I wasn't so naughty maybe they would have stayed together," or "Maybe Mum was upset because I made her late that morning and that was why she had the car accident and died." Young children may even believe their own thoughts made it happen: "I wish you weren't here. . ." Even if your child doesn't say outright that they feel guilty, it's important to let them know that none of what has happened is their fault. They will need a lot of reassurance, and it's something you may have to come back to repeatedly.

Isolation

Like many single parents, children can also feel isolated. Meeting up with other single-parent families, where they can interact with children in similar situations, may help them. More than anything, children need to feel loved at this time and to know that someone really cares about them, particularly if their other parent has ended contact with them. If we are blessed with a supportive wider family of grandparents, aunts, uncles or family friends, we can ask them to help meet that need for our children. And where possible and appropriate, we can ask their other parent's family members to be involved in this too.

Fear of a bad future

When children have been treated abusively, their parent has walked out on them, or one parent has behaved badly towards the other, they can be left with the fear that they won't be able to have a happy relationship themselves. Phrases such as "Like father, like son" or "Isn't she so much like her mother?" may prey on their mind, with the worry that they will turn out the same. If we are concerned that this thought process might be applicable to our children, we can help them realize that it is not the reality. They have a choice about their own behaviour and there is no reason why they cannot have a healthy and successful relationship with a partner in the future.

Bereavement

When our child's other parent has died, it's important to let them talk about him or her and for you to share stories.

There may well be tears, but try not to be afraid of this or prevent it – it's far better for those tears to be shed so that the healing process can begin. Be realistic about your partner and don't make them out to be a saint – to pretend otherwise isn't helpful, especially if you and your children have bad memories of their parent.

We can also help to keep their parent's memory alive whenever possible. It might be by remembering anniversaries or taking them to visit the grave or the place where ashes were scattered. Many families display photos of their loved one around the house and watch videos together from time to time as a way of remembering them.

Children who are bereaved of a parent can also feel an extra sense of loss and anger when comparing themselves with friends from single-parent families who are at least able to see their other parent regularly. Encouraging close contact with grandparents and family members on both sides can go some way in helping to fill that gap.

As their parent, we can feel so bad about what our children have gone through and what they have lost that we try to compensate for this by lavishing them with expensive toys, gadgets, and designer-labelled clothes. Many of us have got into a ton of debt for this reason. (However, if our child's primary love language is gifts, we should make efforts not to deprive them of appropriate gifts that don't break the bank!) We can also be tempted to let them get away with bad behaviour or allow them to challenge the boundaries, because we don't want to be hard on them – we feel they are going through enough. It's an understandable trap to fall in to, but what our kids need most of all at this time is consistency and security. Changing the boundaries now can frighten them and cause even greater instability.

The way forward

As well as the emotions discussed above, some children start to experience anxiety, depression or identity issues. They can also display regressive behaviour, where they typically behave younger than they are or revert to behaviour they've already grown out of; for example, bedwetting, thumb-sucking, whining or being overly clingy and dependent. Getting angry about it or trying to shame your child into acting their age is only likely to prolong the behaviour and cause them more stress. The key here is to ignore children's regressive behaviour and focus on the positives, acknowledging and praising appropriate behaviour and talking to them about how they are feeling. If the regression lasts, or your child's emotional health worsens over time, it would be wise to seek professional help from your doctor or a school counsellor.

You may have heard it said that children bounce back quickly, and it's true that in general they are resilient creatures. Child development specialist Susan Hois says that the negative impact of parental separation can be minimised if the child can live in an environment that is supportive to the grieving process.[16]

This support will include giving children age-appropriate explanations for what has happened, why it has

16   Susan Hois, "Effects of Separation and Loss on Children's Development", Prevent Child Abuse, Vermont (PCAVT). https://pcavt.org/assets/files/Articles/%27s%20Development.pdf

happened and what will happen next. As time goes by, they will learn to adapt, but the best way we can help them do this is by giving them freedom to express and safely channel the torrent of emotions tossing and turning inside them. We need to let them know we want them to share their feelings with us and that it's OK to sometimes be sad, angry, and confused.

When our children have come through painful experiences of family breakdown or bereavement, the emotional love tank we talked about earlier may well have been ruptured in some way. It may be that they don't believe they are truly loved, so using their primary love language will go a long way to repairing the leak that has caused them to feel this way. We can also help them process their emotions by listening with compassion, helping them to face reality, acknowledging their hurt, and empathizing with their pain.

Supporting our children at this time can be far from easy if we are having to deal with the same emotions ourselves. If our own emotional tank is on empty or not being topped up, it's only natural that we might struggle to fill our children's tanks. If that is the case, don't be afraid to reach out for help to work through your struggles in a positive way. Psychologists Sherill and Prudence Tippins put it this way: "The best gift you can give your child is your own emotional, physical, spiritual, and intellectual health."[17]

---

17   Tippins, S. and P., *Two of Us Make a World: The single mother's guide to pregnancy, childbirth and the first year* (New York: Henry Holt & Co, 1995), p. 56.

Chapter 6

PARENTING A CHILD OF THE OPPOSITE SEX

Mums and sons

....

I was so frustrated when my oldest son wanted to shave for the first time – I had no idea how to help him. The poor boy had four or five cuts on his face from trying to use my woman's razor.

JAIME

Sometimes as mums we can feel very insecure about our ability to raise our boys on our own (and the same goes for dads and daughters). We can also worry about them lacking a same-sex role model and how we will get them through puberty and all its accompanying issues. But there's no reason why we can't do a good job. We just need to be proactive and perhaps be prepared to step outside our comfort zone once in a while.

Doing "boy things" together

Not all boys will enjoy doing what we think of as typical male-orientated hobbies or activities, but if they do, spending some quality time with our son doing those things that interest him will strengthen our relationship. My son loved to play on the Xbox, so I used to make the effort to play on it with him. I was rubbish at it, but it was great because he enjoyed it so much. And I remember once going paintballing. I wasn't looking forward to the day – being bombarded by paint pellets was not my idea of a good time – but I ended up having so much fun, and we created some great memories together.

For mums like myself who don't naturally gravitate towards doing what are traditionally thought of as male activities, some ideas for boy-friendly trips include visiting fire or police stations and football stadiums (I took my son to his favourite team's stadium, Manchester United), going to activity centres, sports events, airports, skate parks, bowling, camping or factory tours. Boys can also be interested in music, dancing, singing or drama. The important thing is to find out what activity your son enjoys and do it with him.

Role models

If our son's father has died or his father is not around for other reasons, we can encourage relationships with men who we know will be good role models. They may be grandfathers, brothers, uncles, cousins, friends, club or youth leaders, but they need to be someone we trust.

Sometimes relationships like this don't come about naturally, so we may have to proactively identify people we could ask to help – though making sure that we do not put any undue pressure on them. For instance, if your son is interested in fixing cars or learning to play the guitar, you might want to ask a friend or relative with these interests to give him lessons. Being involved in a sport is also a great way for boys to enjoy the company of other males (I am so grateful to a few of my friends who used to kick a football around with my son), and it's often the case that coaches find themselves in a secondary role of confidant and counsellor. If your son isn't the athletic type, see if he would enjoy going to clubs centred around his interests – anything from scouts to self-defence classes, drama or computing workshops.

"The man of the house"

I wonder if you've ever heard someone say to a boy, "Well, you're the man of the house now." It's especially likely to happen when a father has died, and it's not helpful. Giving our child a role, responsibilities or authority for which they are not qualified or mature enough is a pressure on them that they do not deserve, and can lead to worry, depression, withdrawal or anger. This is not to say that we cannot give age-appropriate chores to our son, but the expectation (either our own or that of others) that he will step into our husband's shoes is unfair and unhelpful. We need to give our son the freedom to be the child he is.

When your children do carry out tasks for you or for other members of the family, make sure not to take it for granted. Showing appreciation and acknowledging the help they give will build their self-esteem and go a long way to preventing feelings of resentment.

Despite our best efforts not to burden them, it's natural for boys to want to be protective of their mums, and if we begin dating again that's something to bear in mind. We'll talk a little more about this in the chapter on dating in Part 4.

In the end, the natural transition from boy to man will take its course and is not something we need to worry about. One of the things I found helpful when my son was going through phases I didn't understand too well was to chat about them to male friends who would give me reassurance.

Dads and daughters

Dads, if you have skipped the above section on mums and sons, read through it now, as there are some similar issues and principles. With regard to adult role models, for example, you would be wise not to go it alone but to find women such as aunts, grandmothers, youth leaders or friends whom your daughter can relate to. Encouraging your daughter to enjoy a relationship with a woman you trust will give her the opportunity to turn to someone familiar when she needs specifically female help and advice.

It can be easier for dads to be more active in their sons' lives because, generally speaking, they are more likely to have common interests, but it's important for you to be involved in your daughter's life as well. Organize playdates for a younger child and take her swimming or to the park. Meet an older child's friends, drive her to sleepovers, look at the photos she's taken – be interested in her life. And in the same way as single-parent mums can intentionally do boy things with their sons, dads can do something fun with their daughters. Ask her where she'd like to go or what she'd enjoy doing. It may well be very different from your idea of fun and you may even feel awkward doing it at first, but push through those feelings and remember *why* you are doing this. You are strengthening your relationship and creating happy memories for you both to look back on. I've seen dads playing dressing-up games with their pre-schooler, going for afternoon tea with a teenager, and having a face mask applied at the spa. Cherish these times together. One day she will be all grown up and fly the nest.

Build her self-esteem

As parents, we play an important part in helping our children develop confidence and a healthy sense of self-worth. Perhaps more than ever before, our kids face the pressures of living up to society's definition of what makes you important and successful in life. Every day as your daughter grows up she will be bombarded by messages that tell her how she should look and dress, and whether or not she is physically attractive. Increasingly, we hear disturbing stories of the damage to fragile self-esteem that can be done so easily through unkind or cruel social media posts and text messages. When we are raising children in such a world, one of the greatest gifts a father can give his daughter (and son) is his affirmation and unconditional love. Sometimes dads can find it difficult to show their love (even if it's what they feel in their heart), but make it a priority to find a way of doing this that works for you. Of course, you need to be honest when giving praise and encouragement – certainly as they grow older, our kids will see through us straight away if we aren't – so be specific and positive: "You are so good at colouring", "You looked after Gran really well when she came to visit", "Your hair looks great today", or "You were so kind to that girl in your class". We know that beauty isn't everything and it's good to remind our daughters that their value and worth goes so much deeper. Let her know you are proud of her. Even if they don't act like it, teenage girls need their dad's approval.

Rob Parsons wrote about this in his book *The Sixty Minute Family*.[18]

> *I've shared some of my failures with you, so let me share a little success. My daughter Katie is married now. I promise you she is one of the least arrogant people you will meet, but she said to me recently, "You know, Dad, I feel pretty confident when I get into new situations, meet new people – just OK about myself. And I realized the other day that since I was small you've said things to me like, 'You look good in that' or 'That meal you cooked was brilliant.' And I realized that the first man in my life accepted me, loved me, and made me feel I was special."*

---

18   Parsons, R., *The Sixty Minute Family* (Oxford: Lion Hudson plc, 2010), p. 33.

Talking versus fixing

It's not good to stereotype, but I think it's safe to acknowledge that many men will have an "I must fix it" attitude: identify the problem and find the solution. There's nothing wrong with that! However, single dads should take on board the fact that girls are more likely to want to talk about their problems and work out their own solutions. This can be hard for a dad whose natural instinct is to tell her how and when to sort it out, or to simply take matters into his own hands and fix it himself. If that's so for you, you will need to have patience and work at the communication side of things by prioritizing time to listen with understanding and talk things through with your daughter.

Having said this, it may be helpful to do a bit of coaching now and again with regard to problem-solving (and the same goes for sons). When your kids have a problem, help them to think through the issue carefully, identify alternatives, and come to a conclusion. Giving them good problem-solving skills and encouraging them not to rely on you for solutions equips them well for adult life.

All parents are protective of their children, but dads can often be especially defensive of their daughters. It's an understandable instinct to want to rescue our kids if they are in trouble. However, if we are *over*protective they can rebel or become too dependent on us. One of the things we suggest at Care for the Family is to "parent children with elastic": letting our kids step away and try new things while being able to bounce back to us for reassurance and comfort. Little by little we can give them age-appropriate responsibilities and allow them to take some limited risks and even make some mistakes. It is the way that all of us learn and mature as human beings.

Helping your daughter through adolescence

There are lots of books, podcasts, and videos out there to help dads who are raising daughters. I watched a tutorial for single dads on YouTube the other day which showed a father how to plait his daughter's hair! And just as I was grateful to have a couple of men friends I could chat to about my son, you'll find it helpful to have a woman to go to for tips and advice about girl things you are totally unfamiliar with.

Coping with a daughter's advance through puberty is likely to strike fear into the heart of any single-parent dad, but you can prepare for it by educating yourself on the basics through books and YouTube videos on adolescent child development. It may be awkward, but it really is important to help your daughter through this transition. A key thing you can do is to make sure she has a female friend or family member she is comfortable with and can confide in, especially when it comes to periods, tampons, and the like.

Remember that your daughter is growing up and will want to be like everyone else in her peer group with regard to boys and dating. Being upfront and honest about the subject will let her know that you realize she is growing up; that you are doing your best and want to help. If you feel uneasy about all this, don't be afraid to tell her. Beware of becoming overprotective, but be proactive about setting some sensible curfews and dating rules, while letting her know that you take her seriously and value her opinions.

It can be very hard for all dads, let alone single parents, to realize that the daughter who was virtually inseparable from them when they were little may now need her own space as a teenager. You may find it upsetting, but remember that it doesn't mean you've lost your place in her affections. So if your daughter is a daddy's girl, make a mental note not to be blindsided by this potential shift in the future – it's normal.

Chapter 7

ROLE REVERSAL

I have spoken to many mums and dads who tell me that one of the benefits of being a single parent is that they and their children have an especially close relationship. This is natural, because so much of our time is spent solely with them. And children in single-parent families can also have extra-close relationships with extended family members or family friends who are often helping to raise them.

But a danger to be aware of when parenting alone is that because we often lack adult company and friends to confide in (we simply don't have time to enjoy and nurture friendships), our relationship with our children can move from that of "parent and child" to "friends". Throughout their lives, however, our kids will have many good friends, but they will only ever have one mother and father. We should not deprive them of that relationship. Being #BFF with our kids may seem a lovely idea – and we can certainly have a close, warm, and friendly relationship with them – but, above all, we need to be their *parent*. We need to be someone who also gives them security, safe boundaries, discipline, and nurture. It means that at times we'll have to accept that we won't be the most popular person in their world. We'll have to say no when they don't want to hear it, and we'll have to follow through on consequences when a boundary has been crossed.

A second danger we face as single parents is to rely too much on our children for our own emotional and practical support – even to the extent that the roles of parent and child are reversed. This is known as "parentification" and can lead to the child's need for care, guidance, and attention either becoming secondary to the needs of the parent or even neglected altogether. Often the child will take on responsibilities they are not emotionally mature enough to deal with. Please don't get me wrong: I am not saying that it's wrong for a child to do chores or give a parent their emotional support occasionally. What I am talking about is when a parent adopts a dependent position in the relationship and the responsibilities placed on the child become too burdensome – their childhoods are stolen as they have to grow up far too soon.

Growing up, something really bad happened to one of my siblings and my mother couldn't cope. The family started to fall apart and she turned to me for emotional support. It got to the point where I felt solely responsible for keeping the family afloat.

KIERAN

Psychologist David Hosier says that there are two specific types of parentification: emotional and instrumental.[19] Emotional parentification occurs when a child has to take on the role of a confidant, counsellor or even mediator between their parents. Instrumental parentification involves the child physically doing tasks for the parent or their family such as cooking, cleaning, paying bills, and looking after their siblings or a sick parent or relative. It goes way beyond chores and into the realm of what the parent would normally do.

Hosier, who experienced this in his own life, recounted how he became his mother's emotional caretaker and by the time he reached his teens she would refer to him as her "Little Psychiatrist".[20] Placing a child into such a role when very young, especially after the breakdown of the family unit when their emotional needs and well-being should be at the forefront of parental care, is developmentally inappropriate. Children put in this position are overburdened and experience severe stress during a period of their lives that should be made as carefree as possible. It can lead to depression, anxiety, inappropriate guilt, and a tendency to have outbursts of anger and rage.

Journalist Sue Carpenter also wrote about her experience with this form of relationship:[21]

---

19   Hosier, D., "Parentification: A closer look at the harmful effects", Childhood Trauma Recovery (21 March 2015). https://childhoodtraumarecovery.com/all-articles/parentification-a-closer-look-at-the-harmful

20   Ibid.

21   Carpenter, S., "When one plus one equals twice the fun", *Daily Mail* online (15 October 2011). www.dailymail.co.uk/home/you/article-2047533/Single-parenting-When-1-plus-1-equals-twice-fun.html

Parents are apt to focus excessively on their child's every move and have high expectations of them. They may overindulge, overpraise or overprotect them. In the absence of a partner, they sometimes share their problems with their child, even lean on them for support. Indeed, some Spoc [Single Parent Only Child] mothers end up emotionally dependent on their son or daughter, and sons in particular seem to take on an overwhelming sense of responsibility. On one online forum, Spoc children reported feeling pressured and suffocated. One child said, "My mother is my shadow. Woe is me."

This situation is not limited to only children; it can also occur when a single parent particularly bonds with one child, perhaps an older child, more than their other children; this is very unhealthy for them both.

It's great to have a close relationship with our children, but a key factor is balance. So I am not saying that we must lie if our children ask us how we are. If they notice we're a little down in the mouth, we can tell them that we're having a hard day. However, what we must *not* do is open up to them about adult issues and use them as an emotional crutch. In particular, unloading our feelings about our ex-partner must be strictly off limits. It doesn't apply to every situation, but remember that mostly, when you are speaking to your child about their other parent, you are speaking about someone they love.

Childhood goes by so fast, so let's do all we can to be a parent to our child and allow them to enjoy this precious time.

Chapter 8

LIGHTEN UP AND HAVE SOME FUN

I learnt to let the little things go as I already have so much on my plate as it is.

JUNE

Friday night was family night and we'd always do something fun. We cooked a nice meal together and watched a film or played a board game. It became my favourite night of the week!

JOSHUA

It's so important to have fun on this journey. Whatever your financial situation is, you can always find something entertaining to do. It might be going for bike rides, taking a trip to the beach, doing arts and crafts, having girlie pamper nights or kicking a ball around in the park – anything your family enjoys doing. Explore local libraries and museums. Read to the children and listen to a story together on a car trip. Put a tablecloth on the lounge floor on a rainy day and have a picnic while watching films. Be silly and play!

As single parents, we can worry so much about what we *don't* have – perhaps not being able to give our children the best toys, clothes, holidays and trips – that we forget to give them what we *do* have. When they look back on their childhood, it probably won't be the expensive trainers you bought them that your kids will remember. It'll be the time you made a tent in the lounge out of old sheets and camped out in it in sleeping bags overnight, telling each other stories, and eating snacks by torchlight!

Part 3

When the road splits: sharing the parenting

Chapter 1

CUSTODY AND CONTACT

As a single parent, you may well be the sole carer for your children. Perhaps you have been bereaved of your partner, perhaps you and your child have never had a relationship with their parent, or perhaps you did have a relationship with them but that has now ended, with no further contact being either allowed or possible. I've spoken to many such parents who say they feel that they are "double parents", and this is a particularly hard road to walk as there is no one to help co-parent or contribute financially to the home. If you are parenting like this, it is vital to surround yourself with as much support as you can, whether it's from family, friends, support groups, your church or other faith groups.

Other single parents, particularly after a divorce or separation, will be either co-parenting (where the children live with them more or less equally) or parenting as the primary caregiver, with their child's other parent having contact rights.

I did my best to link up with my ex-husband re parenting, but it was like banging my head against a brick wall. Even so, I would advise anyone going through the early stages of break-up to encourage the children to see their absent parent regularly.

EMMA

My ex insisted he saw the children in our home, demanding that I went elsewhere, and refused to talk to me at all.

MADISON

Discord over custody and contact is one of the main issues that cause stress for single parents, so we'll want to do all we can to make co-parenting work, not just for our children's sakes but for our own. Many children who are being co-parented following their parents' divorce or separation will have already experienced trauma – especially if the break-up wasn't handled well by one or both parents. There may have been on/off contact with varying schedules or no schedules at all. And there may have been a long period of deliberation before a final decision was made about how contact would work in the long term with the non-custodial parent. An important outcome for me was that our children would see us, their parents (and step-parents), get along. I wanted them to be comfortable when both of us and their step-parents were in the same room, whether it was at a school concert or a birthday meal out.

Our end goal should always be to work in the best interests of our children, even though that may be extremely difficult or inadvisable because of the nature of our break-up or the position taken by the other parent – for example, when a break-up has happened because of abuse or violence.

For many single parents, co-parenting isn't straightforward, so making it work will demand serious discipline and a determination to put aside our feelings and hurts. Often, we can try so hard to do this, but despite our best efforts, our ex-partner refuses to co-operate or has no interest in working with us. This can be incredibly frustrating, especially when we feel they are letting our children down. At times like these, we need to come to terms with the fact that we did the best we could, and move forward. At other times, we may be the one to cause difficulties or mess up when it comes to co-parenting. When that happens it's good to acknowledge our mistakes, be gentle with ourselves, and make a fresh start the next day.

When there is patience, selflessness, and good communication, and when both of you listen to each other and put the effort in, the benefits are well worth it. By working together to create a secure, loving environment for your children, in which they are protected from conflict between you, you can limit the effects of the negative influence that divorce can have on their health and well-being.[22]

---

22   Pedro-Carroll, J., "How Parents Can Help Children Cope with Separation/Divorce", Encylopedia on Early Childhood Development (June 2011). www.child-encyclopedia.com/divorce-and-separation/according-experts/how-parents-can-help-children-cope-separationdivorce

The very best way to manage the break-up of a family, with minimal long-term harm to your offspring, is to support the relationships that each of you has with the children.[23]

If we possibly can, our aim should be to have a civil, child-centred relationship with our ex-partner. For many of us, that might seem far from achievable, but our feelings about our children's other parent are actually irrelevant when it comes to co-parenting. It's not always true (in abusive relationships, for example), but in most cases our ex will never be an "ex" to our children, just Daddy or Dad, Mummy or Mum.

One way of having a child-centred relationship with our ex-partner is to make a clear separation in our mind between the romantic relationship we once had with them and our relationship with them now as a parent. Child psychologist Penelope Leach describes this as "mutual parenting" and says it is the best gift we can give to our child.[24] If we can mutually parent, we will save our children from the fate of being caught in the middle while we use them in the battle to hurt each other. We will be jointly committed to putting their well-being first and protecting them as much as possible from the impact of the break-up of their family.

---

23   Leach, P., "The Vengeful Mothers Who Tear Children From Their Fathers' Lives", *Daily Mail* (2 July 2014). www.dailymail.co.uk/femail/article-2678528/The-vengeful-mothers-tear-fathers-childrens-lives-Britains-parenting-guru-one-unspoken-scandals-age.html
24   Ibid.

When contact is not the best option

> *Co-parenting with my ex was a disaster! He wanted access, but didn't supervise the kids and let them do what they wanted, including driving tractor lawn mowers, lighting fires, driving old cars round the field and firing air guns. It resulted in a few trips to A&E. He also physically and mentally abused our eldest son. I had to take him to court. My son spoke to the police about why he didn't want to see his dad. Thankfully, he was granted his wish.*

RENEE

> *My children have not seen their father for many years as he was violent and there is a court order to keep him away from us.*

APRIL

I have spoken to many single parents who encourage their children to have a relationship with their other parent but the child resists and even gets very upset when they have to see that parent or go to their home. Research has shown that even very young children can have their own reasons for this[25] and if it's happening with our children, we should try to get to the bottom of it. This is especially important if we

---

25   Fortin, J. et al, *Taking a Longer View of Contact: The perspectives of young adults who experience parental separation in their youth*, Project Report (Sussex Law School, University of Sussex, 2012).

have genuine concerns about their well-being when they are with our ex-partner or their family members. Sadly, I have met many single parents whose children need to be kept from their other parent due to physical, mental or sexual abuse.

If your child does not open up to you about their reasons for not wanting to see their other parent, it may be helpful to ask someone you trust to speak to them – perhaps a family member or close friend, social worker or youth worker. This gives them the opportunity to confide in someone else if they feel unable to do so with you. Don't take any risks concerning them being in harm's way, but do all you can to protect them and gain outside help and support.

If you are confident they are not at risk when they are with their other parent and that their resistance to contact is for other reasons, consider asking for the help of a mediator to give them every opportunity to have a healthy, ongoing relationship with him or her.

Keep your child's best interests at the centre when arranging contact

Children thrive on routine and consistency, and when family life has been disrupted those things are even more important – knowing what to expect each day gives them a sense of stability and security. I remember going to a parent/teacher meeting a few months after my husband left. The teacher asked me how my son was doing since the break-up and told me my son had mentioned that he didn't know when he was going to be at his dad's and when he'd be with me. I was totally shocked. I thought we'd developed a routine of my son going to his father's every other weekend, but it seemed that we hadn't communicated this properly to him.

My ex-husband and I had different perspectives with regard to contact. He wanted it to be more fluid, so that the children could come and go to each of our homes whenever they wanted, as he only lived ten minutes down the road, but I felt this lack of routine would affect their stability. I also thought it would be hard to keep tabs on where they were and what they were doing. Someone had to be the main caregiver and they needed to live primarily in one place. Perhaps these differences in our preferences had confused our son, so when I got home I sat down with him and explained that from that point on he could look forward to seeing his father every other weekend. Later on, when he was old enough, he did pop down on his bike to visit his dad at other times as and when the occasion arose.

If we are not the primary caregiver, we can try to be as thoughtful and flexible as we can with regard to contact arrangements. So, for example, if a school sports match or a social event that our child really wants to attend comes up when it's our turn to have them, we can be open to changing the date. If we enforce our rights to contact at times like these, perhaps stopping them from going to things they've set their heart on, it will only make it harder for us to maintain the positive relationship we want to have with them.

Don't put your ex-partner down

....

Speaking negatively about my children's father in their presence damaged my relationship with them and damaged still further my relationship with him.

JO

Many of us have been there: our ex-partner has really annoyed us, we are angry, and when we talk to a family member about it, we accidently let it slip in front of the kids and go off on an emotionally charged tangent of insults. Or perhaps we don't do it accidentally. At some level we *want* the children to hear what their other parent has done. Even if what we're saying about our ex-partner is true, and whether our kids hear it accidentally or not, the end result is that we've put them in the awkward position of feeling torn between the two of us. This might be something we need to remind friends and family about too.

Sometimes an ex-partner can say something negative about us in front of the children and naturally we long to defend ourselves, but even if it takes every ounce of self-control we possess, our best response is to say that we're sorry he or she feels that way and then let the matter go. Of course, that's far easier to read than actually do; however, letting it go is better than having our child stuck in the middle while we trade insults. We can certainly get things off our chest at some point, but not when our children are listening in.

I think it's important to speak to the children positively about their other parent and to find someone you trust to share your frustrations with about how your relationship with your ex is going.

GRACE

When we don't put our children's other parent down, it teaches them that we can still appreciate their positive qualities, despite our differences. My ex-husband was very good with his hands and when my son's bike was broken, I told him that his dad was the best person to ask to fix it – much better than me, in fact. We can also decide not to join in if our children criticize or talk disrespectfully about their other parent (even though, for some of us, it may be music to our ears!).

It's important to keep good lines of communication open with your ex-partner and treat them respectfully. However tempting it may be, never criticize them in front of your child. When you do this you force your child to choose between the two of you, and you risk making them feel disloyal, guilty or angry.

Chapter 2

COMMUNICATE!

M any co-parents enjoy an amicable relationship with each other, and this makes life a lot easier when it comes to contact arrangements and exchanging information about their children. For others of us, however, the most difficult aspect of co-parenting is that it requires frequent communication with our ex-partner, perhaps when we would much rather not have *any* contact with them. Dealing with this isn't easy, and we may need to put in a lot of effort to make it work, but it is necessary if we want our children to enjoy both of us being their parent.

The way in which we communicate with each other affects all our relationships because we can do so in a negative or positive way. In their book *Crucial Conversations – Tools for Talking When Stakes Are High*,[26] Kerry Patterson et al point out that people have three typical responses to dealing with a crucial conversation: (1) they can avoid it; (2) they can face it and handle it poorly; or (3) they can face it and handle it well. The one to aim for, of course, is to handle it well.

---

26   Patterson, K. et al, *Crucial Conversations – Tools for Talking When Stakes Are High* (McGraw-Hill Education: 2nd edition, London, 2011), p. 4.

Patterson et al go on to explain that each of us will enter a conversation with a unique combination of views, feelings, desires, and experiences, and our aim should be for both of us to express these openly and honestly. When people get accurate and relevant information out in the open, it enables them to make better choices and they will act more willingly on the decisions that are made. If one of them keeps their thoughts to themselves, however, they are rarely committed to the final decision – even if they say at the time that they are on board with it. They can end up following it through half-heartedly or not at all, quietly criticizing and passively resisting.

Have you ever had a conversation with your ex-partner that was like this? You thought you'd both agreed on a decision affecting your child, but afterwards they did not follow through on it.

I always wanted things to work for the sake of the children after we separated. Their mother and I would arrange childcare around work commitments and sharing weekends. Sadly, I got used to being let down at the last minute, as she would change her plans. This was really hard for me to deal with. I learnt to not rely on her and to expect the minimum.

CLIFF

The aim of any "crucial" conversation is to benefit our child. So whenever we find ourselves arguing, being sarcastic, verbally attacking, manipulating the discussion or refusing to engage in it, and whenever we show a negative attitude to our ex-partner through our body language and facial expression, we are playing a costly game.

High-stake decisions such as choice of school, holidays, boundaries, and consequences can mean that emotions run strong; so at the very time when we need to be in control of our tongue and our actions, our feelings can run away with us. A key principle of successful conversations is to focus on our desired outcome first and foremost.

Take control of your attitude

When we have a poor relationship with our ex-partner, it's so easy to go into a conversation believing they are the cause of all the problems – "If I could just fix him/her, it would all be better." Perhaps we still feel bitter towards them or, at the very least, irritated. Perhaps we feel the break-up was their fault and they owe us one – they should let us have our way and if they even dare to voice their opinion, we'll be out of there. Or we may deliberately keep information back from them as a way of holding the power balance. I've seen many children miss out on a quality relationship with both their parents because of situations like these.

If you recognize yourself in any of this, it may be a good idea to work on your mindset, your heart, and your attitude before you move on to tackle the relationship with your ex-partner. He or she may well need to change too, of course, but *you* cannot change them; only they can do that. It may be intensely satisfying to let off steam at your ex-partner, and you might feel justified in doing so, but walking away huffing and puffing is pretty worthless when it means that nothing is resolved and you have failed to get a positive outcome for your children.

Don't let yourself get distracted from the main issue

Take this scenario: Emma phones her ex-husband Steve to sort out the travel arrangements for the children when they go to stay with him the following weekend. It should be simple enough to agree, but when Steve makes a remark about her not taking the children to their pre-paid swimming lesson last week, Emma sees red. She'd had to take an elderly relative to the doctor unexpectedly and all the accusations Steve made in the past about her "wasting money" and "not making the after-school activities a priority" now come flooding back.

As understandable as it is for Emma's hackles to rise, rather than sticking to the matter at hand, listening to Steve's suggestions, sharing her own, and coming out with a positive result for the children, Emma's focus immediately changes. *He's unfair and selfish. How dare he say that to me?* she thinks. She finds herself saying down the phone, "Unfortunately, plans have changed for this weekend and the kids are too busy. We'll have to arrange another time."

Remember that it's about having a positive outcome

....

I just do as I'm told. If ever I raise my opinion, it's only shot down anyway, so it's best to just keep the peace.

JAMES

Negotiating effectively is not about winning, punishing others or even about keeping the peace; it's about coming to a beneficial decision for all involved. If you start to go off track, remind yourself what you want to achieve, and refocus your thoughts and the conversation. It may help to write these down so that you have something visual to come back to. Clarify in your own mind the things that you *don't* want to happen – for example, you don't want to walk away with unresolved issues or have your children hurt from decisions that were made as a result of out-of-control emotions. Be creative and think outside the box if you cannot come to a mutual decision.

Communicate in the way that works best for you both

Communication and organization are extremely important when co-parenting, and it's probably easier than ever before in today's world of digital technology, so as single parents we can take full advantage of this. A key component in establishing good communication with our ex-partner is to agree on a method that will work well for us both – it could be physically meeting up, phoning, emails, Skyping or texts. Using online shared calendars such as Google calendar is a great way to co-ordinate schedules, weekly visits, children's school events, and holidays, and they can also create automatic reminders and notifications of regular repeating events.

Other useful online communication tools are Our Family Wizard, Cozi, and 2houses, which you can use to track shared expenses, store up-to-date contact information, create reminders and to-do lists, and keep a separate kids' calendar that both parents can share. They also allow you to track homework assignments and long-term school projects, add shopping lists, plan meals, and keep family journals. MaintainPay is a site that will help you receive, track, and manage childcare payments. You can also record how you or the other parent spend the money that has been given for your child.

I want to leave you with two words of warning about communication. The first is never to make your children the primary source of information to and from your ex-partner. It's up to you to inform each other directly about any changes in your children's lives or circumstances, and to make each other aware of anything they are finding challenging or difficult.

Secondly, as tempting as it might be to ask your children questions about their other parent – who they are dating, what they spend their money on, where they are going on holiday – it's a temptation you should work hard to resist. Why? Because it's so unfair on the children. They may feel you're asking them to spy, and putting children in the middle of adult issues, perhaps relaying news and information between you, can lead to them feeling confused, anxious, helpless, and insecure.

Chapter 3

A UNITED PARENTING STYLE

Children's well-being is greater when both parents have the same approach to discipline and boundaries. So although it may not always be possible, when we are co-parenting, it's far better to agree on a parenting style with our ex-partner if we can. Provided that things were working well on the parenting front prior to our break-up, it's good to aim to maintain the same boundaries as before so that children feel secure about this in a world that has changed so much for them.

All children will test boundaries and challenge the rules, and if we haven't yet experienced our kids playing off one parent against the other, we soon will. It is typical of children in all families, but so much easier for them when their parents live apart: "Dad lets me stay up until . . ." or "Mum said I can play on the computer as much as I like." Co-parenting is all about communication and coming to a happy medium with regard to parenting. So if we're able to agree on routines and discipline, it will help make the transition from one house to the other as smooth as possible for our children.

Co-parenting with someone who has a completely different parenting style from us is a huge challenge – especially if the other parent wants to be a Disneyland mum or dad, where the focus is simply on having fun with the children without giving them any boundaries or discipline. It can make it all the harder for us to enforce boundaries in our home without them seeming strict or extreme. My ex-husband gave our children a great deal more freedom than they'd had when we were together. However, although I was very worried about this, despite our different approach to parenting I have no doubt that my children's father loved them and thought he was doing the best for them – as I did.

I remember asking myself, "Am I being too hard on the kids? Am I too strict? Should I ease up on things?" Sometimes I really had to stand firm and stick to my guns, although it would have been far easier to give in. Often, though, I'd start to question myself and wonder if I was doing the right thing. This is when what I call my "guilt-busting" friends came to my assistance – trusted family members or friends who would discuss my fears with me, give me honest answers, and encourage and reassure me to keep going with what I was doing (if they agreed it was right!). It was often particularly helpful to talk to someone with children a little older than mine – parents who had already been through it themselves.

Having a different parenting style from my children's father meant that we needed to work out our co-parenting with lots of give and take. We had many, many discussions. There were times when we weren't able to come to an agreement and other times when we did. I remember one particular time when we were actually both on the same page. Something was happening in one of our children's lives that we were both concerned about and we met up to discuss it. It was one of the best conversations I'd had with my ex-husband since we broke up. We both wanted the same outcome. He took the lead in sorting the situation out (which I greatly appreciated), and it had a positive, lasting effect on our child's life.

When we can't agree on the boundaries

My ex knows that the kids go to bed at 7.30 p.m. every night, so why does he let them stay up till 9.00 p.m. when they are with him? It's like he's doing this to wind me up.

MICHAELA

There may be times when we can't come to an agreement with our ex-partner, or when they choose not to work with us. When that happens we have two choices: we can allow it to grate on us (risking an outburst or further arguments), or we can bite our tongue and try to live with it. Remember that our children are watching our every move and we need to be examples to them. As long as they are safe and are being looked after by our ex-partner, even if it's in a different way to what we would prefer, we need to leave well alone and accept that when they are with their other parent, they are no longer in our realm of control.

If it's not possible to agree on a parenting style with our ex-partner, we'll need to focus on how we will parent our children when they are with us. It's completely appropriate for us to parent in our own way in our own home, and I continued to have the same boundaries for my children that they'd always had. At times, I was definitely the not-so-popular parent because of it, but good parenting is not a popularity contest.

We've talked previously about choosing our battles and this can be a recurring theme of co-parenting when our child's other parent is more lax than we are. We'll need to decide what issues are the most important to us and be prepared to stick to our guns when they are challenged. If we find ourselves in a battle with our kids about something that isn't actually crucial for us, we can afford a little give and take.

Cyclonic behaviour

When I was co-parenting with my ex-husband, I noticed that although my son's usual behaviour would be fairly "normal" and settled, on every occasion after visiting his father, when he came home his mood would be quite different: stormy and uneasy. I called this "cyclonic behaviour". He would sometimes act up and be moody or unsettled, and it would take a while for him to get back to normal again. No doubt this came about because of the very different routine and boundaries he was experiencing at his father's. The best thing we can do in situations like this is to help our kids return to their routine as soon as possible. Being aware of and acknowledging what is happening is half the battle. If we know they may act up on the night, or even the next day, after they return home, we can prepare ourselves for it.

Shared parenting is often not straightforward – in fact, it can be very messy – but many single mums and dads co-parent successfully. It can take a lot of perseverance, self-control, and hard work, but it can be done – and done well!

Chapter 4

PARENTAL ALIENATION

My ex's family continually interfered with our children. They tried to turn them against me and told them all sorts of lies about me. It was horrible, and I was so hurt and shocked that they would do this to me.

DAWN

A danger to be mindful of if we have had a bitter divorce or separation is a concept known as "parental alienation", where a parent is alienated from their child. It's an increasing phenomenon and occurs when children are manipulated by one parent and/or their family members into disrespecting, fearing or hating the other. In other words, the "target" parent is vilified so much that the children's feelings are poisoned against them and can result in the children unjustifiably rejecting that parent. The usual reason for one parent alienating the other is that they want to exclude them (and even their family members or friends) from the life of their child. They put their own emotional needs first, either by asking their child to take sides and ally with them, or by using the child to make the other parent suffer.

This manipulating behaviour can happen in many ways, ranging from relatively mild to very serious. It may include constantly badmouthing or belittling the targeted parent, limiting contact, forbidding discussions about them, or creating the impression that they dislike or don't love the child. At its extreme end, the manipulating parent will try to force the child to reject their other parent completely. Signs of this happening are when a parent is discouraging contact or visits; not going to an event if the other parent will be there; name-calling; making derogatory remarks about the other parent or their close family so the child can overhear; destroying the child's presents, or things the other parent has made for them; destroying photos; undermining the other parent's parental authority; portraying themselves as the victim in the break-up or saying the other parent was responsible for it; convincing the child that the other parent doesn't love them; making false allegations of abuse by the other parent; telling the child the other parent will hurt them; completely cutting off any communication and contact with the other parent; destroying any physical thing that would connect the child to them; and never speaking about them.

An outcome of parental alienation may be that the child makes up any excuse not to see their other parent and takes on the alienating parent's emotions and hatreds, verbalizing them as their own. It can often lead to long-term or even permanent separation from that parent and other family members, and it increases lifetime risks of both mental and physical illness.[27]

Stop it in its tracks

If, as you read this, you recognize any of this behaviour in yourself with regard to your ex-partner, take a step back right now and think about what it is doing to your children. Until now, perhaps you haven't even recognized what you're doing, particularly if it's one of the less "serious" behaviours. Your ex-partner may have hurt and damaged you, and you may find it impossible to forgive them, but your behaviour means that your children are being hurt now and in the long term. As well as teaching them that it's OK to manipulate and interfere negatively in other people's relationships and lie to achieve a goal, you are putting them in the damaging position of having to choose one of their parents over the other.

As single parents it's vitally important that we lay aside any grievances about our ex-partner and put our children's physical and emotional well-being first. This isn't a tug–of-war battle where one family needs to get the child on their side. It's about giving our children the freedom to spend time with both of us, their parents, and their family members without being bombarded with negative comments. I want to give my heartfelt thanks to my own family for the way they dealt with this issue. No matter what was going on between

27 Bernet, W. et al, "Child Affected by Parental Relationship Distress", *Journal of the American Academy of Child & Adolescent Psychiatry* (Vol. 55, Issue 7, July 2016), pp. 571–79.

my ex-husband and me, they never said a bad word about him to the children and would even ask them how he was doing. That really was putting the children and their feelings first.

When we are the target of parental alienation

Parental alienation, unlike other forms of abuse, isn't always clear-cut, and it can take time to recognize that it's happening. Unlike physical abuse, there are no visible scars or bruises, and children will rarely tell the targeted parent what their other parent has said or done when they are alone with them. This form of psychological abuse can be very subtle in the way it's used in our children's lives, and even teenagers may not know or understand that it's happening.

While we shouldn't be paranoid, we also mustn't ignore signs that we might be a victim of parental alienation. If we find that we are a target, there are different ways to deal with this, which partly depend on the age and maturity of our children. One option is to tackle it head on by speaking to them about what their other parent has said or is doing, and explaining to them why it's happening. Another is to confront the other parent, have a family meeting, or even go to mediation. A third option is to get the help of a solicitor. Family dynamics differ and we'll need to do what we feel is right for our children and ourselves, carefully weighing up the potential positive and negative outcomes.

Here are some things to consider or put in place if you are being alienated from your child:

- Strengthen your relationship with your child. Spend quality time with them. Remind them when you see them how much you love and want to be with them.
- Educate yourself about the issue so that you can identify if and how it is happening.
- If your ex-partner's alienating behaviour is fairly mild, consider whether they are aware that they are doing it. It may be worth having an initial quiet word with them to express your worries and see how they react.
- Recognize that confronting your ex-partner has the potential to worsen the hostility between you. However, if the alienation is serious and recurring, increased hostility may be less of a concern than your priority to protect your child from further psychological abuse.
- Keep a record of every unsuccessful attempt to contact or spend time with your child, keep any returned mail, and list every visit and phone call you make in case you need to provide evidence at a later date.
- Reassure your ex-partner that you are not trying to hurt them or take the child away from them.
- Choose your battles, co-operating and compromising whenever you can.

- Release your child from the pressure to choose. Remind them that they are free to love whomever they want to love, and don't blame them for any rejection.
- Model good behaviour to your child. As much as your ex-partner may be hurting or irritating you, two wrongs don't make a right. Children are smart; they will eventually put the pieces together.
- If the behaviour worsens, consider seeking mediation or legal advice; courts are now taking parental alienation more seriously.

Above all, stay calm and never give up! It's extremely cruel but, sadly, some alienating parents succeed in keeping their kids from the other parent for years, even an entire childhood. You may find that you have to fight a long battle, but *never give up hope*. I know parents who have finally resumed contact with their children as teenagers or even as adults.

Although we may both want what's in the best interests of our children, the niggles and squabbles can be difficult to overcome. If we cannot get past these, we can aim to arrive at a point where even if there is less contact and communication, we are able at least to practise what Penelope Leach calls "polite parenting".[28] She explains: "In polite parenting, there are lesser degrees of contact and

---

28   Leach, P., "The vengeful mothers who tear fathers from their children's lives: Britain's top parenting guru on one of the unspoken scandals of our age", *Daily Mail* (4 July 2014). www.dailymail.co.uk/femail/article-2678528/The-vengeful-mothers-tear-fathers-childrens-lives-Britains-parenting-guru-one-unspoken-scandals-age.html

communication but parents still protect the children from the worst fall-out from the separation."

However, if despite our best efforts co-parenting with our ex-partner is still very difficult, it may be helpful to seek mediation or the advice of a family counsellor to help us gain our bearings and create a relationship where we can both parent our children to the best of our abilities.

Chapter 5

NON-RESIDENT PARENTING

I've found that parents who are not their children's primary caregiver tend to be overlooked as single parents. As well as being my children's resident parent for many years, I was also a non-resident parent at different times in their teenage years when they decided to live with their dad – though not both at the same time. Even when they were living with their father, they used to visit me regularly, so I had to learn to parent differently and also build a different relationship with them. Situations like this aren't easy and sometimes it feels as if we're not fulfilling our role properly as their mum or dad, particularly when we don't see them as frequently as we'd like.

The main thing that helped me in all of this was changing my mindset. As hard as it was, I realized I needed to accept that I was no longer the parent with primary responsibility for my children. I really had to take this on board when communicating with my ex-husband about the children. For that period while they were with him for the majority of the time, it was his parenting rules that had to be adhered to. And during this time, I was paying child support to him rather than the other way around.

Having been both the resident and non-resident caregiver at different times, I have empathy for both positions. I can understand the struggles and frustrations of primary caregivers, and I can also understand what it's like for non-resident parents who don't wake up with their children most days, who see them perhaps every other weekend, and who are unable to arrange their kids' schedules or make sure they get to doctor's appointments.

However, among all the trials and struggles we face when we are non-resident parents, the important thing is our children and that we stay connected to them. We need to ensure they know they are in our thoughts, that we care about and are interested in them, and that we'll always be there for them – in short, that we love them.

Keep in touch

My wife left me for another man and took our two children with her. She now lives a five-hour drive from my house. I only get to have my children for one weekend a month. I miss them so much and think about them every morning when I wake up.

RAY

Staying in regular contact with our children helps to strengthen our relationship and builds their trust. And as the adult, it's our responsibility to make this happen. If we live near enough, we can attend school concerts, parents' evenings, plays and sports events whenever we can to support our children. If this isn't possible, we can note the dates in our diary and be proactive about asking our children how things went, making sure we take the time to listen and show interest in what they are saying. If we can't speak to them face-to-face, a phone or Skype call is a great option.

Although it can be difficult to keep in touch – especially if we live a long way away – communicating from a distance is so much easier today than it used to be. For video chatting, use Skype or FaceTime – this is a great way for you to read younger children a bedtime story. For older children who have smartphones or tablets, as well as Skype and FaceTime you can use email or online mobile photo-sharing sites like Instagram to send photos and send messages via Messenger or WhatsApp. And why not try playing online games such as *Battleship*!

For parents who are rarely able to see their children, a great way of letting them into our life is to keep a journal and send it to them regularly to show them what we've been up to. We can also write our life story (it doesn't have to be a literary masterpiece!) so that when they are older, they'll have something to read that will help them get to know about us a bit more. Writing something like this for our children can also help us when we're missing them or feeling lonely.

Plan ahead

It helps to plan visits with or from your children well in advance so that everyone in the family knows what's happening and there are no misunderstandings. Draw up a schedule with your ex-partner of the dates when you will each have your children. Agreeing and keeping to these is very important. Children learn to trust at an early age, and you can help maintain that trust by keeping your promises. While younger children don't have a true grasp of time, they'll know if you aren't there when you said you would be!

My son was so excited that he was going to see his dad on Sunday. I got him ready and he waited at the door. His dad never turned up and it broke my son's heart. His dad didn't even call to say he couldn't make it. My son cried that whole afternoon.

PAM

Let your children know immediately if you are unable to attend an event or visit when they are expecting you. Children can become deeply distressed and feel rejected if a contact visit doesn't happen, so let them know how long it will be until you see them again and assure them that you love them and can't wait to see them soon.

Make an effort to plan the time you'll have with your children – it's precious and you don't want to waste it. Be respectful of their dislikes, likes and commitments, and try to do things that you all enjoy. Make sure you have a back-up plan in case plan A goes wrong – for example, outdoor activities that may be cancelled because it's pouring with rain.

Routines and belonging

Children feel happier and more secure when they know what to expect, and a structured routine also makes life easier for you. As far as possible, continue with the routines and boundaries they have with their primary caregiver – for example, meal times, bed times, homework and screen time. If you don't know what these are, ask their other parent.

Make sure that your children have their own toothbrush, PJs, mug, slippers and so on when they are with you, so they don't feel like visitors. It's not always possible, but if you can, give your child their own permanent room and decorate it with them, so they know they have a special place in your home that says they belong there. I love how one couple I know did this for the man's oldest child. They lived five hours away from his son but they kept his slippers alongside theirs in the hallway, had a family plaque with everyone's name on it, including his, had photos of him around the house, and they were able to give him his own bedroom, which they decorated with Marvel comics.

Family traditions are important in any family because they give children a sense of belonging and security, so as a non-resident parent, continuing past family traditions and creating new ones is important. Whether it's sitting down with milk and biscuits when they arrive at your house, going out for a cooked breakfast on Saturday mornings, or always going for a trip to the seaside in the school holidays, get some of those traditions going!

Look after yourself . . . and have some fun

When you don't see your children every day, you and they will experience different emotions at different times: sadness, joy, loneliness, guilt, relief, or even all of these on the same day. This is normal, but if parenting apart gives you an overwhelming sadness that persists, it might be a good idea to seek professional help to work through this.

Whatever their passion is, engage them in it and allow them to do the things they enjoy doing. My youngest and eldest loved drama, so I took them to drama club on the Saturdays they were with me. My middle son was crazy about football, so I played football with them all when they were here and went to all his games.

BEN

Whether parenting apart is something you are doing against your wishes or by choice, remember to focus on the quality rather than quantity of the contact you have with your children. When you are with them, give them your full attention. Chat about their hobbies and the activities they like to do, and think of ways to engage with them around these interests. And, last but not least, make sure you have some fun! It's good to laugh together.

Part 4

The climb uphill: getting equipped for the journey

Chapter 1

FRIENDSHIP AND SUPPORT

I felt very alone and isolated. My advice would be to seek those around you who are encouragers and good listeners. If that's not an option, try baby/parent-toddler groups, single-parent support groups or coffee mornings.

JULIA

I've learnt to accept anything offered, not worry about pride, and to seek out any charity support.

TOM

Although it seems impossible at first when we become single parents as a result of traumatic circumstances, the time will come for all of us when we're able to move on from the initial shock and grief. Reaching this point will take longer for some of us than for others, so we mustn't let anyone push us into starting to rebuild our lives before we are ready. During this part of the journey, we'll often take two steps forward and another one back. I remember days when I really felt on top of my game, ready to face the future, then a day later I'd be struggling to get out of bed and get the children to school! Days like this are inevitable. They will come... but they will also go.

Strong social relationships have a positive impact on our health and well-being because of the practical and emotional support they can provide. It is certainly not true of everyone, but men and women tend to behave differently in how they obtain emotional support. On my single-parent journey, I acted fairly typically of women by talking to my family and friends at length – it was my way of processing what I was going through. Ben, a single-parent dad, also wanted company, but it wasn't in order to talk. He told me: "I had a mate who'd come over to visit me once a week to watch a couple of television programmes. All we did was sit and watch TV. We hardly ever spoke. However, that time meant the world to me, and I looked forward to it every week." So although it's not always the case, generally speaking a woman can best be helped by having someone to listen as she talks things through, whereas a man values companionship such as meeting up with a mate for a pint or having a game of pool.

Some people are better than others at asking for and accepting help, and independence isn't a bad trait to have as single parents, because we have to carry the full responsibility of raising our children. However, *none of us can do it on our own all of the time*. We'll all have need of help on occasions, whether it's for a babysitter or practical help around the house if we're down with a cold. So as we begin the climb uphill, we need to strengthen our support network – or start building it from scratch if we don't have one already! This is not calculating – it's practical. Often, people will have no idea what our needs are, so we need to make the decision to tell others if we are struggling. Different friends will be able to help us in different ways according to their skills and the time they have available.

I was totally out of my depth. I had worked away a lot and my wife had pretty much taken care of the house and children – she had a routine in full swing. Little did I know what a luxury it was for me to have such an amazing wife who juggled so many things . . . She woke up one morning, went down to make herself a cup of tea, and collapsed from a brain aneurysm that killed her. One minute I was married and had a partner for life, and the next I was thrown into single parenthood. I had to change my job as I could no longer work away. I needed to be home for the children to look after them. I didn't have the first clue how to run a household.

ALEX

The old saying goes "Give a man a fish, and you feed him for a day; teach a man to fish, and you feed him for a lifetime", so it makes sense to ask friends to help us learn to do things we haven't done before, such as managing credit card statements online, cooking basic recipes, putting oil and water in the car, or setting up filters on our kids' online devices.

One of the best ways to find support and friendship is to go where there are like-minded people: parent and toddler groups, single-parent support groups, church/other faith groups, and community activities. Support networks/groups are also an opportunity to meet up with others going through similar experiences. I used to talk to a single parent online and found her advice incredibly helpful as she was further down the road than I was. Look out for single-parent fairs and websites that can signpost you to helpful organizations.

Loneliness and isolation

Loneliness can just strike out of nowhere with all sorts of triggers.

BEN

I remember after my baby was born all these people coming and visiting, then after four days . . . nothing. I was so, so lonely.

SUE

I'm very lonely. People just don't get it. When people chat away about their partners and families, I feel it then, or even at the school gate. I feel lonely at parents' evenings and at the children's appointments and when I'm dealing with them alone and making big decisions about them. And I feel alone in the evening when they are in bed and I'm exhausted but need to do the chores and there's no one to help.

CLARA

....

The worse days of the year for loneliness are bank holiday Mondays. They feel like nuclear family days. You can't phone your friend; her husband will be home.

YANNA

Having met so many single parents across the country, I can safely say that one of the main issues they struggle with is loneliness. Often, the practical reality of being the sole carer of our children means that we have little time for a social life. But although many of us feel guilty at the thought of taking time for ourselves apart from our children, all parents need a break from the kids now and again, and single parents are no exception. In fact, because we are with them on our own for so much of the time, it's essential that we have time for ourselves occasionally. It doesn't mean we are selfish; it means we are human!

The key to having "grown-up time" is to have it once in a while. It could be a coffee out with friends, going to the pub for a pint, going to an exercise class, visiting a friend at home, joining a choir or an arts class . . . the list goes on.

When we've lost confidence or feel anxious or depressed, the thought of doing something like this can be daunting, so a helpful way to start easing ourselves back into a social setting is to go somewhere where the focus is on the activity. Conversations in settings like this are much more relaxed and can put us more at ease. I asked some single parents to tell me how they had tackled this.

I used to be so lonely at night when the children went to bed. I had no one to talk to. I found Care for the Family's Single Parent Support Facebook page so helpful and joined an online chat room. We all support each other with advice and tips.

SHERRY

My single-parent support group is my lifeline. I look forward to it every week and we even meet up outside of group to do fun activities together.

DENISE

I'd go to the gym and although I may not have gone with friends, I was around people. I'd do an aerobics or other group class so that I was surrounded by other people and never felt alone. I got a buzz out of working with others.

ELAINE

I used to find weekends lonely but have made a network of single friends who are available to hang out with when other friends are doing family stuff. I find the week between Christmas and New Year the hardest and got quite low the first couple of years, but last year I booked a couple of days away at Butlin's, just me and my daughter, and it was THE BEST THING EVER! It was a special time for us and didn't feel lonely at all! I find the evenings can be long, but I now have a Tuesday evening babysitter so I can go out to yoga and see a movie.

TANYA

I have a dog and you very quickly get to know people when you take your dog for a walk – everyone in the park talks to each other.

JEREMIAH

As single parents, let's keep a look out for each other and give each other support whenever we can. Isolation is just as much an issue for dads as it is for mums and can actually be even more difficult to overcome. One dad told me that fathers don't have the same parental networks that mums do, and it's easy for him to feel excluded from social events and even single-parent support groups. Another problem is that men in two-parent relationships simply don't understand what's involved for their male friends who are raising a child alone, let alone do anything to support them.

....

My married friends don't have a clue how hard it is to be a single-parent dad. My mate's wife does everything for him – cooks, cleans and watches the kids. He comes home from work, has his dinner, goes into the lounge and watches TV with a beer. I come home from work, cook dinner, bathe the kids, put them to bed, make the lunches for the next day, clean the house and maybe, if I'm lucky, get to watch a half-hour TV programme when I'm done.

AARON

Sometimes, part of the solution to loneliness isn't people – it's about having purpose. As single parents, we are usually pushed for both time and energy, but if possible, consider volunteering for a charity or helping with community groups, sports or church/other faith group activities. We will need to be wise about how much time we give to this, but there is something special about helping others. Not only does it make a difference to people, but it takes our focus off ourselves and our problems. I remember taking my children to the local foodbank at Christmas to help pack toys for those in the community who had nothing. It was a great activity to do together as a family and gave all of us a different perspective on life. It certainly made us thankful for each other and what we had.

Chapter 2

FORGIVENESS

If we have been abused, rejected or cheated on, hurt and anger are likely to be pretty big features of our lives. And even if we are bereaved, even though we know it's irrational, we can feel anger towards the loved one who left us. We may find that on the upward climb of our journey, well-meaning family and friends start to tell us that we need to let go and forgive. It's certainly true that one of the biggest keys to moving forward and thriving is to forgive those who have hurt us, but as with the other steps on the journey, there's a time and place for this, and it's different for everyone.

I remember speaking to a lady whose friends were pressuring her to forgive her husband who, just weeks earlier, had cheated on her and left her for another woman. She was raw with emotion and nowhere near ready to do that. When we, or our children, have been hurt by someone, most of us will need time – actually, quite a bit of time – to even think about forgiving them. Usually, forgiveness isn't possible until we have dealt with emotions such as guilt, anger, and bitterness. Only then can we begin to think about forgiving that person or even forgiving ourselves (which may be the most difficult of all).

....

Through counselling, I came to the realization that I needed to forgive my ex-partner and his family. I needed to let go of the hate and the anger or else it would engulf me, and I wouldn't be able to move on and care for my son. It was so very, very hard to do, but afterwards things became more manageable.

SALLY

....

It's a process that you start, continue, and keep revisiting. The result is that you have freedom and peace. To hold on to unforgiveness is like being in prison. You are captive to it.

CHRISSIE

When we forgive someone who has wronged us it actually releases us – from hurt, anger and bitterness. When we hang on to anger, the only person who is hurt is us. This hinders us from moving forward and being free. Here are some important things about forgiveness to bear in mind.

1. *Forgiveness doesn't mean that what was done to us is right or that it doesn't matter.* We are not agreeing that we deserved it or that the person who hurt us was justified in what they did, but we are deliberately choosing to let it go and put it behind us.

2. *It's a process.* The hurt won't go away all at once. We'll find that it keeps coming back to us (especially if issues are ongoing), and each time it does, we need to forgive again.

3. *Forgiveness doesn't always lead to reconciliation or mean that we trust the person.* Of course, asking for and giving forgiveness is a wonderful gift that can allow relationships to be restored and healed. But as single parents on the uphill climb, our lives will have moved on, and renewing a couple relationship may not be possible, desirable or the best option in the circumstances. Forgiving our ex-partner (or others) also doesn't mean that we become a doormat or accept ill-treatment from them. We need to set boundaries or limits regarding the behaviour we accept from others – we'll talk about this later.

....

I forgave my husband for leaving me for someone else, but I still don't trust him. He continues to lie and has shown that he hasn't changed, as he left his second wife in similar circumstances. In forgiving him, I was able to let my ex-husband go and continue with my life without bitterness.

EMILY

....

In time, I was able to forgive my ex for what he'd put me and our children through. It took time, lots of time, but I feel that I have finally come to a place

where I can honestly say I have forgiven him, and I
feel so free because of it.

JACKIE

So how do we do it? The way that worked for me was by speaking it out, often through gritted teeth: "I choose to forgive . . ." After doing this repeatedly, I found I started to mean it and, in time, I began to feel it. Eventually, I began to forget. You may be reading this thinking, "How on earth could she *forget*?", but knowing the Hebrew meaning for the word "forget" really helped me to understand this process – it means "to wither". So although we will never completely forget what has happened, it will cease to dominate our lives, thoughts, and actions. Forgiveness means that we can move on without the chains of anger and hurt pulling us back.

Chapter 3

MONEY, MONEY, MONEY

After paying bills, I have around £20 a week to spend on food for my three children and myself.

KIERA

During the summer, I cannot claim anything and cannot work due to childcare problems, so I have to make a small amount go a very long way. I eat one meal per day, we have no holidays or days out, and birthdays are particularly difficult times. I have been doing this for three years now.

SHIRLEY

We became poor almost overnight and had to leave our home. We struggle financially, but I've learnt to live frugally. There's not much help for people who still work and have a mortgage, but going on benefits would mean I'd lose our home.

DANIELLE

....

*I work and only earn enough to survive. There's no
extra money for any luxuries, not even to take my
children to the movies now and again.*

FAITH

A relationship break-up or bereavement affects us in so
many different ways, and for many single parents it
includes our finances. When my marriage ended, I had no
income at all – I had just left my job and was about to start at
university, and my ex-husband was the main breadwinner.
I had to think quickly as to how I would bring in an income
and survive financially. If our partner was the one who dealt
with the family finances, this can be an overwhelmingly
scary issue to deal with initially. Many single parents have
told me that they don't know where to start; they don't know
what they are entitled to in the way of benefits and have no
idea where to go for help.

Statistics show that nearly seven out of ten single parents
work (which should dispel quite a few misconceptions!)[29]
However, single parents have the highest poverty rate
among working-age households.[30] There are many reasons
for this, including the cost of childcare and the fact that it's
increasingly difficult for many single parents to find work
that fits around caring for their children and pays enough to
lift them out of the poverty trap.

29   Rabindrakumar, S., "One in Four: A Profile of Single Parents
in the UK", Gingerbread (February 2018). www.gingerbread.org.uk/wp-
content/uploads/2018/02/One-in-four-a-profile-of-single-parents-in-the-UK.
compressed.pdf
30   Ibid.

There's no easy solution when it comes to money issues, but one of the strategies to use on the climb uphill is to *take control*. By this, I mean making ourselves fully aware of our financial situation. When we're staring the figures in the face, we can start to deal with staying on top of them. This may well be very unfamiliar territory and some of us are better than others at dealing with finances, so if that's the case for you, I urge you to get some help. I can't cover this adequately in the space allowed by this book, but in the appendix I have signposted you to places where you can get advice and support.

Learning to budget is essential to being in control of what you spend and what you have coming in. Of course, if you are struggling to make ends meet, you can't magically make money appear and, sadly, for many single parents, even after cutting back on spending as much as possible and carefully budgeting, there is still nothing left over to meet basic living costs. Again, if this is your situation, I urge you to seek help in finding out what benefits you are entitled to.

For me, having a family budget was key to helping me get back some control. And if you are in debt, or about to fall into debt, it's crucial that you don't put your head in the sand and ignore it. If you're not sure where to start, a debt advisor can really help. Make sure you go to a reputable organization for *free* advice.

If you are divorced or separated, make sure that you notify all banks, credit card companies, store cards, catalogues, lease-hire companies, and so on that you want your partner's name removed from all accounts. This will protect you from being liable for any debts that your ex-partner has incurred.

It's OK to say no

Sometimes as single parents, we can find it hard to say no to our children when they ask us for things or want to do activities that we can't afford, and when we *do* say no, we feel guilty. Of course we don't want them to miss out on the good things in life, and if they have been through a painful time we may feel that we can "make it up" to them through gifts and treats. But although saying no can be tough, in the long run it's far better for them that we don't get into debt and get stressed because of it. We'll also be modelling to our kids how to be financially responsible. Don't forget that the greatest gift we can give our children is our *presence*, not our *presents*.

Chapter 4

KNOW YOUR LIMITS – STRESS AND WELL-BEING

Looking after children alone as their primary caregiver or co-parent is exhausting. We're juggling so many things, both physically and emotionally, that it's no wonder many of us feel worn out.

Taking care of our own well-being is usually the last thing on our priority list – our children come first. And looking after them is a 24/7 job. Where do we find the time? But in the long run, neglecting our own welfare isn't good for anyone.

....

Don't forget to look after yourself, because your health matters for the sake of your children!

STEVE

....

I ended up crashing with crippling anxiety and being signed off for a few months.

DEBBIE

No spare time

Critical and judgmental of self

Exhaustion

Poor housing

Financial difficulties, low income, breadwinner

No one to talk to

Juggling act of work, housework, kids

Isolation and loneliness

Feelings of guilt and judgment

Lack of sleep

Co-parenting

No social time to relax

Lack of practical help

No alone time

Entering the dating scene again

Can't spend enough time with the kids

No one to share things with in good and bad times

No one to make us feel loved

When the safety instructions are announced before take-off on a plane, the flight attendant always gives the same advice: in an emergency, put on your own oxygen mask before you help your children with theirs. Why? Because you'll be in a much better position to look after them if you can breathe! And it's exactly the same principle when it comes to our general health and well-being. I learned this lesson the hard way. Some days, I felt I was only just keeping my head above water. I was mentally, physically, and emotionally exhausted by the work, pressures, and anxieties of single parenthood. I'm not alone in this.

The truth is that there are no easy answers. Yes, it's crucial that we accept offers of help with alacrity when they come (so don't forget about building a good support network), but the reality is that all too often we have to cope without help when we need it. It's especially difficult if we can't afford childcare, holidays or babysitters.

I eventually learned to "grab" time for myself whenever the opportunity arose. If I knew I needed to slow down, I'd have a PJ day on the sofa watching movies with the kids. I was still spending time with them, but I was resting. When I was married, I loved having a facial or massage and it really upset me that I couldn't afford it any more, especially because I felt it was something I needed more than ever. I started going to a college and having a treatment done by students – I went from paying £70 for a massage to £15. I saved that £15 through the month and guarded it with my life because I knew it was important to me – it rejuvenated me. Facials and massages may not tick your box, but the principle is to do something that really gives you a boost, mentally, physically or both.

I enjoy painting and when my son is having his afternoon nap, I pull out the watercolours.

JOY

I put music on in the kitchen and dance around. It always puts a smile on my face.

LISA

When I'm angry or stressed, I like to write – it seems to help when I can put things on paper.

MARY

Single parents frequently experience high stress levels, with a consequent decrease in well-being, so learning how to "de-stress" is important. A big part of this is about identifying your limits and taking heed of warning signs that those limits are about to be reached. There are a number of options when that happens:

1. *Stop what you're doing.* When the children are squabbling and you've juggled a million different things since early morning, missed your dentist appointment because of a childcare crisis, need to cook dinner, and have what feels like a drill inside your skull, the amber warning light is flashing and it's time to stop and regroup. Dinner can wait. Whether it's putting a movie on for the children and retreating

to your bedroom with a cup of tea for half an hour or getting the kids together and going out to the park for an hour, find what works for you and do it.

2. *Offload*. Whether it's phoning a friend, messaging them or going to visit them, tap into your support network and chat. Be honest and let people know how you are feeling.

3. *Allow yourself to do nothing*. It's easy to feel guilty if you're not being busy, but the truth is that even if you were on the go every minute of every day, there would still be more you could do. I remember a friend telling me, "Kat, the housework can wait, but your health and well-being can't." I really took this to heart and started to realize that I could stop – it was OK. Whether it's reading a magazine, playing a computer game or just drifting off to sleep on the couch in the afternoon sun, do it once in a while. You'll feel better for it.

4. *Ask for help*. Be proactive about seeking help when you're under pressure. Identify what you need most help with (someone to watch the children, the housework, running errands) then ask for specific help with it. I struggled with this terribly at first, until I learned that my independence was hindering rather than helping me. If routine household chores are a big stress for you, don't be afraid to hand out a limited number of age-appropriate jobs to your children. Always be aware when they too are under pressure, but if they *are* able to help you when you have a million and one things to do, it will also teach them responsibility and make them feel part of the family team.

5. *Be realistic.* The pressure we put ourselves under as single parents can be crushing. We are trying to be a mum *and* a dad, and we want to be the perfect parent for our children, but physically, mentally, and often financially, that's just not possible. Make up your mind to do the best you possibly can, but accept that anything beyond that you will just have to let go.

6. *Say no to unnecessary commitments.* It's good to recognize that there are seasons in life and that while you are raising your children you need to prioritize your time. When they are older and have left home, you should have more free time to take on new commitments.

Get organized

I can guess what you're thinking: "Organized? When do I have the time to get organized?" I sympathize, but I want to mention this because for me at least, taking the time to bring a bit of order into the chaos of life helped reduce my stress levels so much. Start small, tackling one area at a time, and gradually extend it to more and more parts of your life. If being organized doesn't come naturally, you'll need to be proactive about taking these practical steps, but it will be worth it.

Here are some ideas:

• Make the kids' lunches for school, lay out their uniforms and pack their PE kits the night before, so there's not such a panic in the morning.

- Plan menus for the week ahead and bulk cook at the weekend.
- Write to-do lists to help you remember what needs to be done – important things first and not-so-urgent things near the bottom.
- Create a realistic schedule for you and your family. Put the essential activities in first (for example, work, school, homework), then prioritize extra activities according to how important they are to you all. Don't forget to allocate time for yourself and the kids to chill out and relax at home. If you find you are doing more activities than you can keep up with, be prepared to cut down on these.

Boundaries

....

I meet my ex to exchange the children in a public place that has cameras, to keep him from continually assaulting me in front of the children.

LARISA

....

My ex-wife left me for another man a couple of years ago. She continually asks me for money and tells me that she can't make ends meet, even though she gets paid more in her job than I do in mine. I am the primary caregiver of our children and she doesn't give me any child support. I constantly give her money and know I need to put some financial boundaries down with her, but I find this hard because I don't want the children to see their mother suffering, and I think I still have feelings for her.

JAKE

One of the ways in which we can protect our well-being is to have what psychologists call boundaries: conscious, positive and healthy ways to protect ourselves from others' harmful behaviour. Personal boundaries set limits for acceptable behaviour and help people in all sorts of relationships to be mutually respectful and caring, but I believe they are particularly significant for single parents because old boundaries can easily be blurred. We need to reassess the boundaries we now want to have with our ex-partner, family, and friends, and put new ones in place if necessary. These will allow us to set clear expectations for how we want to be treated and what our ex-partner or others can expect from us in return.

Many single parents can feel they don't deserve to have personal boundaries, particularly if they have a low self-esteem, but we *all* deserve to be treated with respect. Boundaries are especially helpful in protecting us from people who don't have our best interests at heart or who may try to exploit us.

We all want to be "nice" people, to give and take (especially important when we are co-parenting), and for some of us it's very hard to say no to things, because we don't want others to think badly of us, or perhaps we're fearful of what might happen if we do. But if we are to survive and thrive as a single parent, we need to be clear about the line between doing something because we *want* to and being taken advantage of.

If we are divorced, we don't have to take on the responsibility for solving our ex-partner's problems, even if we still care about them. And likewise, we should stop relying on them for emotional support, turning instead to trusted friends and family. Boundaries help us make the break a clean one and stop us from getting frustrated; they establish the rules for how we will now interact with each other. Of course, in some cases, where we're on good terms with our ex-partner, we may feel that our relationship is such that we can support each other as friends, but even here it is helpful to have clear boundaries about personal issues.

Here are some of the boundaries it may be important for you to consider.

Physical boundaries

- No physical contact at all with your ex-partner if there is a danger of physical abuse. If necessary, this may require measures such as a restraining order.
- Meeting only in a public place or with friends.
- Not allowing them to use their key to let themselves into your home or turn up unannounced.
- Not allowing them to go through your things or help themselves to food in your home.

Emotional and practical boundaries

- Not doing jobs for your ex-partner, such as cooking meals or fixing things around the house.
- Not trying to sort out their problems.
- Not going to your ex-partner for emotional support or letting them come to you for it.
- Not allowing them to verbally or emotionally abuse you.
- Not looking at their social media posts and photos – resisting the urge to "snoop" on what they are up to, and closing any joint social media identities

Co-parenting boundaries

- Not giving in to requests from your ex-partner to drop off and collect the children each time the children go to them.
- Not letting it become a habit for them to bring the children back late, or only have the children when it suits them.

Financial boundaries

- Not allowing maintenance payments to be made late, missed occasionally or never made. This may mean asking the Child Maintenance Service to intervene.
- Not giving your ex-partner money or loans.

Having boundaries is not about being deliberately awkward, uncooperative or vindictive. Even if your end goal is for your children to have as good a relationship as possible with their other parent, you also have to ensure that you don't make your life impossibly difficult and stressful because you can't say no when you need to.

When you're still recovering from a traumatic time, you shouldn't expect too much from yourself too soon; so, if necessary, start small with boundaries, perhaps by addressing one behaviour at a time. Let me give you a warning, though! Initially, when you lay a boundary down, you may find that your stress levels go up if the person concerned doesn't like it. This reaction is normal, so stick to your guns – get moral support from friends, family, youth leaders or others whom you trust.

Boundaries are important in all our relationships, so as well as those we have with our ex-partner, we can put them in place with our ex-partner's family and mutual friends.

Chapter 5

FINDING YOURSELF AND MOVING TOWARDS THE FUTURE

Sometimes in life, people can feel that their identity is like a ship sunk at sea, and that's certainly true of single parents. Perhaps we've taken on a brand-new role as a parent, or after being one half of a couple for many years, we've suddenly become *me* again rather than *us*. We may find ourselves asking questions such as "Who am I?", "What does society think of me?", "Do I see myself as others do?", and "Am I a failure/a victim/a hero or heroine?"

It's important to recognize that the circumstances we're in are not the *whole* of us. Before I remarried I was a single parent, but it was only ever *one* part of me, not the whole. If you'd spoken to my family or friends, especially my children, they'd have told you a lot more about me than that I was a single parent. They'd have told you about my personality, the things I love to do, my talents, and skills – and the things I'm rubbish at!

Whether or not we wanted to be on the single-parent journey, we can survive and thrive by accepting who we are now. We can't control everything in our lives, but we *can* choose to honour ourselves; and, in doing so, we can find ourselves once again. As the saying goes: "Be yourself. Everyone else is taken."

For many of us, it may mean we have to dig deep to rediscover our identity. I love socializing and having friends round, but wasn't able to do this as often as I would have liked when I was married. So as part of finding a new identity after my break-up, one of the things I started doing was hosting friends again. I held a movie night at my house on a Friday night and once had thirty people in my lounge to watch a film! I loved every minute of it – it was *me*.

Identifying who we are is a process. Here are some simple questions to ask yourself, to help it along:

- What do I love to do?
- What makes me happy?
- What makes me feel good?
- What things would I like to do?
- What do I like to read?
- What music do I like?
- What do I want to learn?
- Who do I like to spend time with?

At a single-parent weekend event I ran, one of the mums said she'd been reminded that she used to love painting. She hadn't done it for years and decided to enrol in an art class. Whatever our passion or interest is, we can make it a big part of our single-parent journey.

Building your confidence

I felt worthless and that there must have been something wrong with me or we'd still be together. My self-esteem was at rock bottom.

TRUDY

I have such low self-esteem now since my husband left me for another woman that I struggle with the thought of dating again. I mean, who'd want me now?

MARTHA

I am constantly second-guessing myself when I've done something, and I'm paranoid about getting it wrong. I'm not sure I can make any good decisions any more after all that's happened.

JACOB

....

I never feel good enough. I put myself down, and I feel I'm not worth looking after.

AMY

A relationship break-up can badly affect our self-esteem in a number of ways. We may feel rejected by someone who has left us or cheated on us, and we may even feel that we don't deserve happiness; that we are worthless or not good enough. We may feel responsible for the break-up of our family or even guilty about things that were not our fault. When relationships have gone badly wrong we may have had a number of painful things said to us (even by ourselves!) and the danger is that these can become our truth. One single parent told me that she'd travelled the world alone before she got married, but her experience of divorce caused her to lose so much confidence that she found it hard even to come on one of our single-parent family holidays. To every single parent out there, let me say this loudly and clearly: you *are* worth it! We all are.

The encouraging thing to remember is that low self-esteem and confidence is not a terminal condition (even if it's always been a problem for us). A key to combating it is to identify and challenge negative thinking and actions: "Do I think or say negative things about myself?", "Do I spend time with people who put me down/depress me?", "Do I automatically assume I can't accomplish things?" Next time you feel bad about yourself or feel that you've messed up, question whether you'd speak to someone else in the same way you are criticizing yourself. And then consider whether you want your children to think and feel the same way about themselves as you do about yourself. If we want our children to have confidence in us, we must first show them that we have confidence in ourselves. And to help them grow up with a healthy self-esteem, we must model that.

Single parents don't have a partner to encourage them through the challenging moments (hours, days, weeks!) of raising children, so it can be difficult to deal with negative thoughts. And when we're physically and emotionally exhausted, any feelings of inadequacy we have are heightened. A great way of combating this is to decide to focus on the positives. Pat yourself on the back for the things you've achieved today, both big and small. And congratulate yourself for organizing that picnic at the weekend and for doing the weekly food shop when you'd rather be anywhere else in the world than in the supermarket!

Deliberately focusing on the many ways in which you are caring for your children every day, and capturing all the negative thoughts before they take hold, will help you build up a true picture of your own value. While we shouldn't let ourselves off the hook when we really do mess up, we need to accept that none of us is perfect – even single parents! All healthy relationships are about accepting and forgiving each other, including our relationship with ourselves.

Don't compare yourself to others

If we aren't careful, we can live our lives constantly looking over our shoulder, wondering what other people think about us, comparing ourselves to them and then feeling guilty, inadequate or a failure if, in our eyes, we don't match up to them. But the truth is, they are different (we all are!), and we have a responsibility to do things in a way that works best for us and our family. If getting the children off to school in the morning is just about all we can cope with at the moment, the last thing we should do is look sideways at other parents.

I remember visiting a friend and staring round in dismay at her spotless house. How did she do it? I love a clean, tidy house, but when I'd left home that morning – running late – there were piles of dishes in the sink and stacks of laundry waiting to be washed. I was juggling too many things at once, something had to give, and the majority of the time it was housework. Years later, I found out that my friend had a cleaner! In the end, I decided that I could only do what I could do and that quality time with my children was more important. Another friend said to me, "Housework will always be there, but one day your children will grow up and leave home." Boy, was she right! I took that on board and never compared my house to anyone else's again.

Seeing through positive glasses

It's about looking at the positives. Yes, my washing machine leaks, but I have one and it cleans our clothes. And practising thankfulness. Compared to many in the world, I have so much.

KIM

> *In making an effort to think good, positive thoughts and learning to look after ourselves, we are making "deposits" in our lives rather than "withdrawals".*

SAM

We've all heard about the power of positive thinking, and it's true that our outlook and attitude – whether we're generally optimistic or pessimistic – has an effect on the quality of our lives, either positively or negatively.

Often we need to be proactive about making "good" things happen in our lives. Try sitting down when you have a free five minutes and asking yourself what you'd like to happen in the future. Once you've done that, consider what small steps you could take today to start you on the road to achieving those things.

Now, I can hear some of you saying that this is pie-in-the-sky kind of thinking – it's irresponsible not to keep our feet firmly on the ground – but I'm not talking about living with our head in the clouds and pretending that setbacks and difficulties don't happen. What I'm saying is that intentionally trying to have a positive mindset helps us get through the hard times and stay motivated to work towards a hopeful future. A quote from Rocky Balboa, the title character in the 'Rocky' film series, who had to overcome huge challenges in his life and career as a professional boxer, made a real impact on me. He talked about being knocked about and beaten up by life, but said that winning wasn't about how hard you got hit. It was about how hard you can get hit and keep moving forward. For me, the message – to keep moving forward – is the key to surviving and thriving on the single-parent journey.

When I first became a single parent I was in so much pain that I'd wake up crying and go to sleep crying. But it didn't stay like that for ever. The day came when I realized I needed to look to the future. I am a Christian, and it was a verse from the Bible that helped me: "'For I know the plans I have for you,' declares the LORD, 'plans to prosper you and not to harm you, plans to give you hope and a future'" (Jeremiah 29:11). Suddenly I realized that I *could* have hope. I did have a future and that future could be a good one. I decided to write a bucket list of the things I'd always wanted to do in life. Some were small; others were bigger and would take years to accomplish. One by one I started to work towards ticking those items off the list. It gave me a focus, and every time I achieved one, it boosted my confidence and happiness. The first thing on my list was learning to swim. I'd always thought I couldn't float, and the day I did, well, it was amazing! One other thing took me years to achieve. I went back to university and got a degree. The feeling on graduation day when I walked up to get my certificate, then stood with my children to have our photo taken, was incredible.

I can think of so many other single parents I've met in the last few years who have come through their challenges and are now doing things they'd never imagined possible. A mum who went on one of our Take a Break activity holidays regained her confidence so much that she did a Return to Practice course and re-entered the district nursing profession. She then went on to start a single-parent support group and a drop-in foodbank.

I don't want to minimize all the difficulties you face as a single parent, and I'm not saying that these goals and dreams are easy to achieve. Some will be short term, some medium term and some long term. They may change over the years and you may find you have to put some of them on hold for a while. But every time you achieve a goal, no matter how small, it's a cause for celebration. Have hope for a good future and keep moving forward.

Chapter 6

THE DATING SCENE

I had a fling straight after my break-up, which was a huge mistake. You don't realize it at the time, but even though the loneliness is often excruciating, you have to heal before you can move on to a new relationship.

LAURA

I don't want to date. Everyone else's solution for me is to get on a dating website. I want to do more long-term things.

LESLEY

I tried to find someone else to fill the emptiness inside, but then I realized at the last minute that it was not the right reason to be with them.

DAWSON

Very quickly I started to have another abusive and controlling relationship. Fortunately, I saw the light and ended it. Now I am in a happy loving relationship. It's taken me a long time, but I know he is a nice, caring man.

DEBBIE

I'm quite happy to be on my own and not the slightest bit interested in getting a date or a boyfriend.

LUCY

"To date or not to date?"

Among those who are on the single-parent journey there will be some who dismiss the question immediately, some who put it on the back burner for the time being but remain open to the possibility of dating in the future, and others who are ready to give it a go. Some single parents have told me they've been put under pressure from others to start dating, but it's important not to give in to such demands, even if they are low-key. Only we will know when the time is right. It may be a long time before we're ready (if we want to at all), and if we do want to go ahead, it's important to do so for the right reasons.

Dating is always a bit of a minefield, but now that we have children it's a very different scenario from when we were footloose and childfree. As well as our own needs and wants, we have those of our kids to consider. And there are practical challenges, of course. Do we have the time and energy for dating? Who will look after the children?

Imagine the scenario:

- *Phase 1*: Spend afternoon on phone finding another babysitter after yours drops out at midday. Feed, bathe and put children to bed. Get dolled up. Run through with babysitter everything the children are likely to need. Hand over emergency phone numbers and address of restaurant. Breathe. Spray on favourite fragrance. Pull up Spanx/male equivalent. Breathe. Leave.
- *Phase 2*: Nail entrance walking up to date at the restaurant. Say hi. Get seated. Begin date.
- *Phase 3*: Nod off midway through main meal. Come to with a jerk. Check to see if date noticed and refocus on conversation. Try to ignore the million and one things whizzing around inside head that need doing on return home so kids are ready for the next day. Feel eyes close again. Make excuse for declining coffee. Leave restaurant. Get through front door. Collapse in heap on the sofa.

Is all that hassle really worth it? On my first date with my now husband, my son was at his father's house. Halfway through the evening, my ex-husband rang me to say my son wanted to come home. I had to cut the date short and shoot off.

But let's not be unremittingly gloomy about the problems of dating; they are challenging at times, but not insurmountable. If we take time to prepare and get organized, go into it with open eyes and avoid the pitfalls, it can be a lot of fun! There isn't space in this book to fully examine the issue of dating and remarriage, but we'll take a quick look at some of the key things to consider.

Am I emotionally ready?

A constant theme of this book has been the need to take time to work through our feelings at each stage of the journey, and hitting the dating scene is no exception. After a break-up or bereavement we are vulnerable emotionally, so it's vital to avoid rebound relationships or dating simply because we're lonely or don't like not being seen as part of a couple. If our self-esteem has taken a heavy blow, we'd be wise to give ourselves time to recover, rebuild our confidence, find our identity, set new goals and grow strong. If we are unhappy with ourselves and carry emotional baggage from the past, there's a danger that we'll make unwise choices or be taken advantage of. In effect, we'll be setting ourselves up to fail in a new relationship before it even starts.

What's best for the children?

It's common for single parents to suffer guilt pangs when leaving children with a babysitter for the evening, but we shouldn't feel guilty about dating – there's nothing wrong in wanting some adult company. And remember that taking care of our emotional well-being helps our children too, because they have a happier mum or dad! On the other hand, before we decide to date we do need to ask ourselves seriously whether it's the best thing for our children right now. If it's better for them that we don't, we may have to make the difficult decision to put our romantic life on hold, at least for a while.

If you do decide to date, talk to your children about how they feel. Be sensitive to their feelings and remember that a child who loves their other parent won't want to hear about how much nicer this new man/woman is than their father/mother.

Don't rush into introducing your new partner to your children. Being presented with their parent's latest date can be very confusing for them. It gets particularly difficult if they like the person and start building up expectations of having them in the family before you are anywhere near that stage. When you feel a relationship has become serious enough, introduce the children to your partner, but keep everything low-key. For example, rather than doing something where the focus is entirely on the new person, go out with them and the children on a trip or activity you can do together.

Older children can have different reactions to you dating; they may simply be glad that you are happy, they may be jealous or protective of you, or they may worry about their other parent's feelings.

Be selective

Your children are something to celebrate, and you want to be with a new partner who will celebrate them too. If your date views the fact that you have children in a negative or half-hearted light, they are not the right person for you. Look for someone who sees your children as a positive benefit rather than as baggage. As one single parent put it, "Having a child helps you sort people into a 'worth it' and 'not worth it' pile early on."

While you are dating someone, remember that parenting your children is your job alone, not theirs. Letting them jump into parenting your children too early in your relationship is not appropriate for them and disruptive for your children. Give your partner and children plenty of time to grow close and develop a relationship as friends before your partner takes on co-parenting duties.

As a relationship grows more serious, constantly ask yourself about your partner's qualities. Are they a person who will be good for both you and your children? Are you confident they have the qualities and skills to take on the important role of co-parent in your children's lives?

There are so many issues involved in dating and remarriage as a single person, not least fears to do with self-worth, trust, and being hurt again. Talk through these issues with trusted friends and family, and don't be afraid to get counselling if you've reached an emotional barrier that you just can't cross. I have been writing this chapter just six weeks after my wedding to my new husband. It was a wonderful day and I am filled with hope for our future. But if I told you about the worries, fears, what-ifs and moments of self-doubt I went through – along with the anticipation, excitement, hopes, and joy – it would take at least one other book! Dating and remarriage is certainly not for everyone, and there's no right or wrong about whether or not to do it. But whatever you decide, hold on to an important truth: your past doesn't have to dictate your future.

Chapter 7

YOU ARE MORE IMPORTANT THAN YOU KNOW

My mother was a wonderful woman who was a homemaker for most of her life. She was married to my father until the day she died, and she raised six children and worked incredibly hard doing so. I can honestly say that she was an amazing mother, not just because she was *my* mother, but because she really was. I learned so much from her example growing up; she lived out her faith, loved us, and taught us to love others. Why do I tell you this? It's so that you will never disregard or play down your role as a parent. It is one of the most important roles anyone can have in life. We have the privilege and responsibility of nurturing another human being during the foundational stages of life. As a parent, you are more important than you know.

Some of us may have had a far from happy upbringing, but we can turn the tide and usher in a different kind of family life for our children and their children. If you're feeling out of your depth with regard to parenting, don't be afraid to reach out for support (see appendix for further information).

There will be many times on this journey when we'll need to be brave and step outside of our comfort zone. I was once that single parent who used to cry herself to sleep at the bottom of the valley, but I climbed back uphill again and reached the top. And if I can do it, I know that you can too. Your goals for the future will be different from mine but, like me, you can meet them by chipping away at them day after day, month after month, year after year.

Athletes endure a lot to get to where they want to go – their training involves blood, sweat and tears. They can see the prize ahead of them and they move on towards it. As single parents, whether or not we chose to be on this journey, we *can* choose to run towards the goal of giving ourselves and our children a wonderful life and a future full of hope.

....

I found myself again through this journey. I am stronger than I thought and more capable. I am enjoying the ride and have fresh hope for the future and lots of goals to accomplish.

JEN

We worry so much as single parents about how everything is going to turn out, both for our children and for ourselves. Yes, we'll have many low times, but we'll also have highs – days where we can laugh with our children, have fun, and enjoy watching them grow up.

When the journey is hard, try to remember that the days of childhood are so short. At the time, you think the sheer slog of life as a single parent will never end, but for me now, it seems that I blinked and both my children were grown. So take a step back and remember to enjoy every minute you can with your children.

Speaking of her personal mission in life, author Maya Angelou said that she wanted not merely to survive, but to thrive. But she didn't leave it there. I love the fact that she went on to say how she wanted to achieve this: with humour, passion, compassion and style. I hope that this will be true for all of you who are walking the single-parent journey. Remember... there is *always* hope!

APPENDIX

Further information and support

The following organizations offer helpful advice and support on some of the issues covered in this book. As specific web addresses change from time to time, it may be necessary to search for the relevant information on an organization's home page or a general web browser.

Single parenting

Care for the Family – Single Parent Support
www.careforthefamily.org.uk
Articles and resources for single parents, signposting to events, groups, and helpful organizations.
Tel: 029 2081 0800

Gingerbread
www.gingerbread.org.uk
Information, advice, policy, and campaigning for single parents and links to local support groups.
Tel: 0207 428 5400

One Parent Families – Scotland
www.opfs.org.uk
Advice and information, services, policy, and campaigns.
Helpline: 0808 801 0323

Singleparents.org
www.singleparents.org.uk
Information, expert advice, interactive learning, multimedia content, links to other support organizations, and news for anyone who is parenting alone.

Additional needs

Care for the Family – Additional Needs Support

www.careforthefamily.org.uk

Articles and resources for parents who have children with additional needs, telephone befriending, and signposting to helpful organizations.

Tel: 029 2081 0800

Contact (For Families with Disabled Children)

www.contact.org.uk

Advice, online information, workshops, medical information, signposting to local support groups for families with children with a disability.

Helpline: 0808 808 3555

Family Fund

www.familyfund.org.uk

Provides grants to low-income families raising disabled and seriously ill children and young people for items and services that they could not otherwise afford or access.

Tel: 01904 550055

Mencap

www.mencap.org.uk

Services for adults and children with learning disabilities, ranging from round-the-clock care to helping someone join in with local leisure activities, providing advice and information on things like employment and education, and helping someone to live independently for the first time.

Helpline: 0808 808 1111

Scope

www.scope.org.uk

Works to bring about equality and fairness for disabled people and provides practical advice and emotional support. Services include a helpline, online community, employment services, and community engagement programmes.

Helpline: 0808 800 3333

Counselling

British Association for Counselling and Psychotherapy
www.bacp.co.uk/about-therapy/we-can-help/
Information about therapy and how to find a safe and effective counsellor or psychotherapist.
Tel: 01455 883300

Relate
www.relate.org.uk
Relationship counselling for individuals and couples, family counselling, mediation, and children and young people's counselling.
Tel: 0300 100 1234

Samaritans
www.samaritans.org
Confidential support for anyone who needs to talk. It doesn't matter who you are, how you feel or what has happened.
24-hour helpline: 116 123

Bereavement

Care for the Family – Widowed Young Support
www.careforthefamily.org.uk
Articles and resources for those who are widowed young, telephone befriending, events, and signposting to helpful organizations.
Tel: 029 2081 0800

Cruse Bereavement Care
www.cruse.org.uk
Confidential face-to-face, telephone, email, and website support after the death of someone close, including services specifically for children and young people.
Helpline: 0808 808 1677

At a Loss

www.ataloss.org

Signposting to local bereavement support, resources, training, and projects, including specific resources for men and teenagers.

WAY Widowed and Young

www.widowedandyoung.org.uk

Social activities and a peer-to-peer support network for anyone whose partner died when they were young.

Survivors of Bereavement by Suicide

www.uksobs.org

A self-help organization that aims to provide a safe, confidential environment in which bereaved people can share their experiences and feelings, so giving and gaining support from each other.

Tel: 0300 111 5065

Domestic abuse

The National Domestic Violence Helpline

www.nationaldomesticviolencehelpline.org.uk

A national service run by Women's Aid and Refuge, for women experiencing domestic violence, their family, friends, colleagues, and others calling on their behalf.

24-hour helpline: 0808 2000 247

NSPCC (National Society for the Prevention of Cruelty to Children)

www.nspcc.org.uk

A national charity to help children who have been abused to rebuild their lives and protect children at risk. Provides advice and support online or via the telephone helpline and can take action on your behalf if a child is in danger.

Helpline: 0800 800 5000

End of a relationship

Advicenow
www.advicenow.org.uk
Clear and effective guidance on dealing with law-related issues,
including separation and divorce.

Cafcass (Children and Family Court Advisory and Support Service)
www.cafcass.gov.uk/grown-ups/parents-and-carers/divorce-and-separation/
An independent public body promoting the welfare of children and
families involved in family court. Resources include a helpful online or
printed "Parenting Plan" to help parents work out the practical details
of parenting after they separate.

Child Maintenance Options
www.cmoptions.org
Impartial information and support to help separated parents make
decisions about their child maintenance arrangements.

Child Maintenance Service
https://childmaintenanceservice.direct.gov.uk/public/#
Self-service website for those who pay or receive child maintenance.
Tel: 0800 171 2345 (GB) or 0345 266 8978 (Northern Ireland)

Family Mediators Association
www.thefma.co.uk
Information about family mediation and signposting to local
mediators.
Tel: 01355 244 594

National Association of Child Contact Centres
www.naccc.org.uk
Neutral places where children of separated families can enjoy contact
with their non-resident parents and sometimes other family members
in a comfortable and safe environment.
Tel: 0845 4500 280

Only Dads

www.onlydads.org

Support for parents who are looking to make the best decisions for their family during separation and divorce. Includes free access to a national network of legal and media experts.

Only Mums

www.onlymums.org

Support for parents who are looking to make the best decisions for their family during separation and divorce. Includes free access to a national network of legal and media experts.

Sorting Out Separation

www.sortingoutseparation.org.uk

A free online resource for parents and couples dealing with divorce or separation (part of the government's Help and Support for Separated Families initiative).

Finances and debt

Citizens Advice

www.citizensadvice.org.uk

Independent, confidential and impartial advice on money and legal matters.

Tel: 03444 111 444 (England); 028 9023 1120 (Northern Ireland); 0808 800 9060 (Scotland); 03444 77 20 20 (Wales)

Christians Against Poverty (CAP)

www.capuk.org

A national debt counselling charity offering support, hope, and a solution to anyone in debt, through its unique, in-depth service.

Tel: 01274 760720

The Money Advice Service
www.moneyadviceservice.org.uk
Information and advice on all aspects of money management and debt, including financial arrangements when going through divorce and separation.
Tel: 0800 138 7777

The Money Charity
www.themoneycharity.org.uk
Education, information, and advice on money management.
Tel: 020 7062 8933

StepChange Debt Charity
www.stepchange.org
Expert debt advice and debt management to help you tackle debts.
Tel: 0800 138 1111

Turn2us
www.turn2us.org.uk
Help to access benefits, grants, and other support for people in financial hardship.

GOV.UK
www.gov.uk
Information on all government services and entitlements, including benefits, childcare and parenting, housing and local services.

entitledto
www.entitledto.co.uk
Online benefit calculators to help determine what you can claim from national and local government via self-serve calculators.

National Debtline
www.mymoneysteps.org
Debt advice by phone and online, including a My Money Steps tool, web guides, fact sheets, and sample letters.
Tel: 0808 808 4000

Housing

Shelter

www.shelter.org.uk

Advice and practical assistance for people in housing need, including threat of eviction.

Tel: 0808 800 4444

See also: GOV.UK (*www.gov.uk*), Sorting Out Separation *(www. sortingoutseparation.org.uk)*, and Citizens Advice (*www.citizensadvice. org.uk*).

Mental health

Anxiety UK

www.anxietyuk.org.uk

Support for those living with anxiety and anxiety-based depression, via an extensive range of services, including one-to-one therapy.

Tel: 03444 775 774

Mind

www.mind.org.uk

Information and advice for those with mental health problems.

Tel: 0300 123 3393

Sane

www.sane.org.uk

Confidential emotional support, guidance, and information for anyone affected by mental illness, including families, friends, and carers.

Tel: 0300 304 7000

Parenting

Care for the Family

www.careforthefamily.org.uk

Marriage and relationship, parenting, and bereavement support through events, resources, training, and volunteer networks. Includes support for families with additional needs, those who are widowed young, single parents, and bereaved parents.
Tel: 029 2081 0800

Dad Info

www.dad.info

Advice and support website for fathers.

Family Lives

www.familylives.org.uk

Help and support in all areas of family life.
Helpline: 0808 800 2222

Home Start

www.home-start.org.uk

Volunteer befriending and support for families with children under five.

Netmums

www.netmums.com/parenting

Social network of parents across the UK: articles, local information, and links to helpful organizations.